a SANE WOMAN'S GUIDE TO RAISING a LARGE FAMILY

Mary Ostyn

GIBBS SMITH

TO ENRICH AND INSPIRE HUMANKIND

Salt Lake City | Charleston | Santa Fe | Santa Barbara

To John,

my high school sweetheart, the love of my
life, my biggest fan. With you by my side,
no dream is too daring.

First Edition
13 12 11 10 09   5 4 3 2 1

Published by
Gibbs Smith
P.O. Box 667
Layton, Utah 84041

Orders: 1.800.835.4993
www.gibbs-smith.com

Designed by Dawn DeVries Sokol
Printed and bound in the United States of America
Gibbs Smith books are printed on either recycled, 100% post-consumer waste,
or FSC-certified papers.

Library of Congress Cataloging-in-Publication Data

Ostyn, Mary.
  A sane woman's guide to raising a large family / Mary Ostyn. — 1st ed.
      p. cm.
  ISBN-13: 978-1-4236-0451-8
  ISBN-10: 1-4236-0451-2
  1. Mothers—United States. 2. Family size—United States.
  3. Parenting—United States. 4. Family—United States.
  5. Ostyn, Mary. I.
Title.
  HQ759.O885 2008
  649'.1—dc22
                          2008029492

Contents

Acknowledgments

I'd like to acknowledge my agent, Angela Miller, who believed in this project from the start; Christopher Robbins and Hollie Keith of Gibbs Smith, who understood and respected what I had to say; my mother, Hazel, whose stellar example as a good mother has been my guiding light, and my father, Dale, who taught me the importance of using just the right word; Ron, who became my dad when I thought I'd never have one again; my daughter Amanda, whose steady calm is an anchor in our busy home; my daughter Erika, whose work ethic and attention to detail amazes me; my son Jared, whose mad computer skills saved me many a document; my son Daniel, whose creative word usage heralds the next generation of Ostyn writers; my daughter Lidya, who cooks like a pro but still likes to sit on my lap; my daughter Zeytuna, who loves running errands with me, no matter how many stops we make; my son Joshua, whose dedication and determination remind me of myself; my son Ben, whose wit makes me laugh even when I'm not expecting it; my daughter Emily, whose radiant smiles never fail to warm my heart; my daughter Julianna, who will always be my "baby" even when she's all grown up; and God, who loved me enough to send his son for me.

GROWING A FAMILY

Are We Crazy to Want Another Baby?

"How can there be too many children? That is like saying there are too many flowers."
—Mother Theresa

I sit in my cozy living room, rocking my toddler as she drops off to sleep in my arms. The chair creaks. The fire crackles. A few minutes ago my teenaged sons efficiently cleared the remains of dinner, and my sixteen-year-old daughter tossed the last laundry of the day into the washer. Appliances now hum with blessed purpose.

My husband is lying on the floor, reading bedtime stories to everyone who cares to listen: first a Bible story and then a chapter from a Narnia book. Younger children crowd around him like a litter of puppies, alternately listening and poking nearby siblings.

The teenagers have brought their own books to the living room to read during the younger children's story time. Now and then they look up from their books and listen to the more exciting bits of the story my husband is reading.

I sit thinking of tomorrow's Thanksgiving plans. The air is rich with the delightful smell of apples and cinnamon, betraying the presence of two pies in the oven. The pies were made this afternoon by my teenaged son. My eighteen-year-old daughter added the final touches to the crust. My son, though willing to assemble the pie, felt that pie primping was too much to ask of him.

Thinking of tomorrow's meal, I'm glad for the thirty-five peeled potatoes gleaming in a bowl of water in the fridge. The under-twelve set peeled every single one this afternoon so we'd have less to do tomorrow.

As I sit soaking in the happiness of the moment, hearing and smelling and seeing and touching my family all around me, I am struck by the peace of it, the warm glow in this house so rich with loved ones. My Thanksgiving has already begun. At moments like this, parents of large families know without a doubt we're the richest people in the world.

What Is It Really Like?

When most people think of life in a big family, they picture haggard moms in desperate need of a referee's whistle. They imagine dads mortgaging their souls to Safeway. They envision enough laundry to fill the Grand Canyon.

I'll admit it: there are moments where my eardrums throb and I wish for noise-canceling headphones. A hefty slice of my husband's paycheck does get chewed and swallowed. And the laundry? In a month I'm guessing mine would fill a good-sized swimming pool.

But the decision to grow your family consists of much more than adding up noise and groceries and laundry, and gauging your tolerance of each. You also have to factor in the multiplication of hugs, the many more funny sayings, and the additional joy of witnessing each child succeed at each new phase of life. I think most parents would agree that a single lisped "I love you" at the right moment can easily outbalance a bathtub full of laundry.

So how do you tell if you have what it takes to parent another child or two? How nuts—or how saintly—do you have to be?

Confession time: when someone asks me how many kids I have and the number "ten" comes out of my mouth, I sometimes still feel faintly

> The decision to grow your family consists of much more than adding up noise and groceries and laundry, and gauging your tolerance of each. You also have to factor in the multiplication of hugs, the many more funny sayings, and the additional joy of witnessing each child succeed at each new phase of life.

surprised myself. After all, I swore as a teenager that I'd never have more than four. My husband and I didn't set out to have a mega-family, and we certainly didn't imagine that we'd end up with six adopted children. But we are so glad to have been led this direction in life.

My husband and I are still very much in the thick of this parenting journey. At the writing of this book, our kids ranged in age from three to twenty. But already we've been so blessed by our experience that we'd love to encourage other families considering stepping out on this adventure. The purpose of this book is twofold:

- To help you decide if you have what it takes to parent another child or two
- To equip you to more effectively tackle the job of raising a busy family

I write from a mother's point of view, and many references in this book reflect that. But the vast majority of this information is usable by dads as well. So if you are a dad reading this book, welcome! This book is for you too.

Do You Have to Be a Saint?

Right off the top, let's tackle that Mother Teresa myth. Thankfully,

> Thankfully, sainthood is not required or else I'd
> have been excommunicated years ago.

sainthood is not required or else I'd have been excommunicated years ago. However, the last time my kids played "dump and mix" with every board game we own, I did think—just before my head flew off—that a little more patience would be handy at times.

While sharing trials and joys along my own journey to mega-motherhood, I'll talk about the issues families face. What if you and your spouse are having a hard time agreeing about your "ideal" number of children? What if your relatives think big families are nuts? Could you meet the needs of multiple children without drowning in sheer neediness? Will your finances stretch to include more children? How is parenting a large family different from having just one or two children?

Here's the quick answer: not only is it possible to raise a large family without going broke or crazy, it can also be a joyous, deeply satisfying adventure.

What Will People Say?

When my husband and I announced our first pregnancy, people were full of congratulations. Announcement number two was greeted with equal joy. The third time around, the celebratory champagne was noticeably absent. Instead came questions.

"Is this it?" people asked. "Are you going to quit if you get your boy?"

Several times we even heard the snide: "You know what causes that, right?"

It amazed me that just three children put us in a whole new category in people's minds. Jill, a mother of four children, had a similar experience:

I wonder how many times I have heard the question, "Are you done?" in regards to my family size. This question and other comments like that began immediately after my second child was born. The nurses crooned, "Ooh, look! Now you can stop. You have a girl and a boy."

Most people assume you have children to check the girl and boy box on your life checklist. It is still acceptable to have three children, but only if the first two are of the same sex. If you would want to have more than that, well, you are downright crazy.

Some people will come right out and call you crazy. More tactful souls will think of ways to ask without quite asking.

"Won't you be glad to be done with diapers?"

"Aren't you glad you're not nursing anymore?"

"Isn't it nice that your kids are getting so independent?"

The questions can get tiring. Once we broke the half-dozen barrier, however, people started to lose hope that we'd make normal choices anytime soon. They began to opt for the resigned but still curious, "When are you going to do it again?"

I've wondered why people seem so interested in another family's choices. In many cases I think they're simply seeking to validate their own choices. A large family disturbs folks; it makes them reexamine their own choices.

The decision to be done with babies stirs deep emotion. Usually there's no do-over. If you reach fifty and find yourself mourning the speed at which parenthood passed, you've probably missed your chance to jump back on the train.

Women revisit the issue many times over their reproductive years. Jen was one of those women:

When we got married, I said, "Two! That's it." My husband said,

"I'd love to have four, but we'll just wait and see." Ten years later, we have a wonderful two, a girl and a boy, everyone's idea of a perfect family. But God has changed my heart. I know we are not done. I know we have children waiting for us. My two has turned into four, maybe more.

Many Christian families are surprised to discover that even their own mothers worry about their family expansion plans. Elizabeth Elliot, missionary and inspirational writer, confessed to struggling with the news of her daughter's pregnancy:

When I learned that my daughter Valerie was expecting number five, my insides tied themselves in knots. Val and Walt were both very peaceful about it, willing to receive this child as they had received the others—as a gift from the Lord.

But my imagination ran to the future and its seeming impossibilities—"Poor dear Val. She has her hands more than full. What will she do with five?" Before she was married, Valerie had told me that she hoped the Lord would give her six. I had smiled to myself, thinking she would probably revise that number after the first three or four.

Practical considerations rose like thunderclouds in my mind. Money. Another room to be built onto the house. Homeschooling (Valerie was teaching two already!). How would the new child receive the attention she needed? Why all this turmoil in my soul? Well, because I loved my child! She was tired! Her hands were full!

Elliot went on to find peace with the thought of this new child, and by the time the baby arrived, she was greeted with joy by everyone, including Grandma. But many women report similar reactions. Relatives often need time to get used to the idea.

Not only is it possible to raise a large family
without going broke or crazy, it can also
be a joyous, deeply satisfying adventure.

Handling Comments

Even when Great-Aunt Millie's comments are made in love, it hurts to
think she doubts your ability to corral or kiss or clothe a few more kids.
When you're just beginning to think about growing your family, fearful
comments can make you doubt yourself. Of course it is wise to hear out
concerned loved ones and to consider their thoughts.

But don't forget it is your own decision, not Aunt Millie's. Parents
of large families do best if they develop a certain sturdiness, a self-
confidence; it comes in handy for the kids and for the comments.
In the end you have to think it through, make your best decision, and
go forward.

Once the newest arrival is a real child, not just a resource-sucking
shadow-figure in your relatives' minds, Aunt Millie will likely be won
over. As for the fear of slack-jawed Wal-Mart greeters spotting your
crew and counting out loud—are you really going to give them power
over your family size?

The fear of going too far, of being overwhelmed by sheer numbers,
is very real. What if the addition of two more muddy feet and one more
soccer schedule and another runny nose proves too much, pushing a
previously functional mommy into talking to herself and wringing her
hands in a corner?

A few years ago my sister and I were talking. I had six children at
the time, and she had just given birth to her second. She declared she
was done with babies and glad of it.

"How can you say that?" I asked, feeling like an alien investigating terrain that made sense to everyone but me. I couldn't imagine ever being so certain myself.

"I don't know." She shrugged. "I just don't want any more."

As it turned out, my sister's certainty was temporary. She and her husband went on to give birth to a third child and then adopted a fourth. No doubt that she had been done on the day she spoke it so certainly, but things change.

John and I know all about that. Back when we were eighteen years old and talking about getting married, neither of us guessed our family would grow to include ten children. As one of three kids, my husband was picturing having two or three. I declared with the infinite wisdom of a teenager that I'd never have more than four. Listening in on our plans, God must have smiled.

On a recent evening, John and I were lounging on the couch, talking and reading and enjoying the sleepy peace that descends after children reluctantly shuffle off to bed. I found myself studying his profile and thinking about our younger selves.

"If you'd known we were going to have ten kids, would you have run away screaming?" I asked.

He snorted. "Probably."

"But you're glad you didn't run, right?"

His lips twitched and his eyes twinkled. "Usually."

That's when I whacked him on the side of the head with the couch pillow.

That's also when I decided it wasn't the best time to confess my recent heart-twinges over our baby turning three. Not that he would have been shocked. I have a long history of lobbying for just one more child.

Finding Agreement

The issue of spousal agreement is huge. What if you want another child and your spouse doesn't? Or you may be a couple for whom the dynamic is reversed. However the disagreement plays out, it is an incredibly emotional, painful issue to sort out. When John and I wrestled that beast, it was the toughest time of our entire twenty-two-year marriage and the first time when I actually thought, "This is why people get divorced. This is the size of problem that does it."

Don't get me wrong: when we got married, we committed forever, no matter what. That resolve didn't falter. But for a little while I was unhappy enough that I understood the desperation that drove people to divide up the CDs and thumb through the *Yellow Pages* for divorce lawyers.

We decided soon after the birth of our fourth child that our family was complete. Our two boys and two girls seemed perfect. But when my baby turned three, my arms began feeling empty. That third birthday is hard for me.

Unfortunately, John was still very much done.

Up to this point John and I had been inseparable, two against the world. We didn't get along perfectly, but we had a knack for understanding each other's dreams. I expected no less this time around. When I shared a new dream of mine, to adopt a baby, his vehemence floored me.

"Are you crazy? Don't you think four is enough? Adoption is expensive. We don't have that kind of money!" he said.

I approached the argument a hundred different ways, trying to prevail with logic and tears and whatever else I could think of. But it was like talking to a mailbox. In the past, when we'd disagreed, we'd always been able to find some middle ground. But this time there was no such thing.

When I finally faced the fact that he was not going to change his mind, I did what I should have done in the first place. I left him alone and instead of nagging began praying. I prayed not only for the baby I so desperately wanted but also for what I wanted even more— unity. I wanted our happy marriage back.

My husband was relieved. In the resultant quiet he began to actually think about it. Questions came, which I'd answer, affecting a nonchalance that I was far from feeling. Could he really be considering it?

When John asked me what I wanted for Christmas, I told him all I wanted was his fingerprints for the criminal background check, the first step in the adoption process. He smiled, unsurprised, and I wondered again if he could really be considering it.

But in the next weeks there were worrisome moments too, the normal moments all parents have, with kids fighting or vomiting or hunting lost shoes. At times like that, he would turn to me in a huff saying, "We don't need another one!"

Several times during December he asked me to expand my Christmas list, probably hoping I would request a slow cooker or a computer instead of a child. I stubbornly asked only for his fingerprints.

By Christmas Eve, my stomach was all in knots. In the midst of four kids ripping gifts open with single-minded delight, John casually tossed a tiny gift my way. With trembling fingers, I opened it. Inside was a little gold key chain with a coin-shaped gold medallion on it that read: "God Keeps His Promises."

I forced enthusiasm into my voice to thank John. Maybe I'd asked too much. Maybe all the hints of the previous weeks were just a fabrication of my hopeful heart. Maybe that dream child was not meant for our family.

But John was still watching me. Finally he said, "What's on the back of the key chain?"

Heart thudding, I flipped the medallion over to look at the back.

There, etched in the smooth gold on the medallion, was a single golden thumbprint.

Never have I loved my husband more than I did on that day when he understood the dream in my heart and made it come true. Even better, once he committed to another child, he went forward wholeheartedly.

Seven months later, when we walked off that airplane with our new Korean son in our arms, John's smile was just as delighted, and his tears of joy just as real as my own.

Two years later, we brought home our second son from Korea. During the next seven years, we also brought home four daughters from Ethiopia. It is amazing to think of the miracle it took to make our family look like it does today.

The issue of spousal agreement is huge. What if you want another child and your spouse doesn't?

Dealing with Your Spouse's Concerns

The issue of the reluctant spouse is common. Husbands especially tend to need time to think before going forward with another child. Men often feel the financial burden more keenly than women. They want to provide for their families. They want to protect them from harm.

Sometimes when my husband goes bodyguard on me, it raises my hackles. I see his protection as an insult to my intelligence. Does he really think I'm helpless? I forget that God has given my man those protective instincts.

One night recently, I got up to use the bathroom and discovered that a door to the backyard was wide open. Every hair on my body went electric with fear. The first move I made was toward the bedroom to wake up John to come investigate. It turned out to be nothing more than a windy night and an unlatched door. But it got me thinking: I'd been so quick to call him then. Why do I resist so much at other times?

When John was dead set against having another child, the welfare of our family was like Mount Everest in his mind. He was not about to leap before he tested the depth of the water. He wanted to keep us safe.

I saw his reluctance for awhile as a faith issue; I was sure John wasn't trusting God enough. I realize now it was just as much about my faith as it was about John's. I had no trouble trusting God for the finances of a larger family. But I didn't trust that God could speak to my husband's heart.

Trust. That's really what God wanted from me all along. He wanted me to trust that he could bring us into agreement. He wanted me to trust that he would not let us miss out on the children he had for our family.

Thinking back, I realize that two things were key to our finally finding agreement. First of all, John and I began to pray together—not that the other person would change, but that we'd find agreement. During that time, I had a verse on the bulletin board above my computer. "And I will give them one heart, and one way, that they may fear me for ever, for the good of them, and of their children after them" (Jeremiah 32:39).

Even as I prayed, I feared that the only way we'd ever agree was if I gave up my dream. Yet that Bible verse seemed also to be a promise for the children, both the ones we already had and those who would be coming to us. So I finally reluctantly handed that dream off to God, still nurturing a thread of hope in my heart.

The second key to finding agreement was even tougher. I decided to quit nagging, to be quiet, and to leave John alone. Over those months of disagreement, my nagging only dug him deeper into his foxhole. He was so busy warding off my verbal assault that he couldn't hear anything else. It wasn't till I was quiet that he could begin to hear that "still small voice" from God.

In talking with other women, I have heard the same two keys repeated over and over. Heather has four children, including two from Ethiopia. She says her husband took quite awhile to warm up to the idea of having more than two children:

Here's my two cents as a wife who has been there. First,
don't nag! Second, don't nag! Third, don't nag! Fourth, pray,
pray, pray.

I am such a doer and a fixer and a mover that it took me months to get to that point. It is hard to leave your dreams in other hands, even when those hands are so much bigger and more capable than your own. But it is so worth it.

Will I Ever Feel Done?

These days I still wonder occasionally if our family is complete. A while ago I happened across my beloved baby carrier sitting on my dresser and realized it had been months since I'd used it. I decided I really ought to hand off the carrier to my sister who had just had a new baby, and tossed it into the van to give it to her at church.

When I got into the van on Sunday and picked up that familiar wad of soft cloth, my stomach clutched in grief. When I'd tucked my toddler into that carrier last, I hadn't realized that was the last time she would ride there, so cozy and happy against my body. Was she really the last baby I'd ever have?

All the way to church I sat with my stomach in knots, clutching that wadded cloth. Could I really bear to give it away? I told myself I was being silly. I knew my feelings weren't so much about the carrier as they were about being done with babies.

When I got to church and coaxed myself to hand it off to my sister, I told her outright I was just loaning it. "I might ask for this back next week," I warned.

My sister understood and assured me that was fine. Truthfully, I did want to share it with her. Just don't make me say I'm finished having babies.

Don't get me wrong. I'm not sure I want more. At this moment

Each time we have adopted, we have not done
it out of some misguided savior complex but because we
wanted another person to hug at night, another
face at our table, another little one to teach to talk and
walk and ride a bike, another person to rejoice
over as she or he grows and learns.

I'm very content with my ten. We now have four boys and six girls, all beautiful healthy kids. Our two most recently arrived daughters were nine and eleven years old when they arrived at our home. Helping them settle in has been an all-consuming job lately. Raising ten children is a huge responsibility, and even I know we can't keep adding forever.

But I've been to Ethiopia. My time there changed all my preconceived ideas about logic and good sense and need.

I've walked through orphanages where child after child plucked at my clothes, raising their arms to be held, wanting nothing more than someone, anyone, to call their own. I've seen babies sleeping two to a bed. I've heard the stories of children who've lived in orphanages for years, praying that some day they would be part of a family again.

At this moment as I sit here on my leather couch, tapping away at my computer, nibbling chocolate, with my children tucked away in their comfortable bedrooms, I know there are tens of thousands of children all over the world dying inside a little more each day because they have no one. I also know how little time it takes a former orphan to become a sassy, self-assured, much-loved member of a family. That metamorphosis is miraculous and delightful to behold.

When people say, as they always do, that our children are blessed, I agree. But instantly I add that my husband and I are equally blessed.

We are privileged to have each of our children and also to live here in a wealthy country.

It's hard for most Americans to fathom true poverty, the kind where parents raise families on $120 a year in houses no bigger than toolsheds, and sometimes realize that it's time to take their children to the orphanage, quick, before the parents die and leave the child-rearing to the neighbors.

I know I'm not solely responsible for the world's children. Each time we have adopted, we have not done it out of some misguided savior complex but because we wanted another person to hug at night, another face at our table, another little one to teach to talk and walk and ride a bike, another person to rejoice over as she or he grows and learns.

And yet, when and if my husband and I declare that finally we're done with diapers, night waking, tantrums from two-year-olds, and potty puddles found when we're in our sock feet, whether we care to face it or not, we are also closing a door in the face of a real living child waiting somewhere in the world who could be ours.

Call me nuts if you will, but I'm not ready to close that door. Not just yet.

Thinking It Through

If you're considering adding a child to your family, ask yourself a few questions. Have you and your spouse prayed about this step? Are you in agreement? Each time John and I have added to our family, God worked unmistakably to bring our hearts into agreement. We just don't agree that easily on our own.

Ask yourself if doors are opening financially. Each time we decided to move forward with another child, we were amazed to see how the money appeared. We truly were witness to miracles. May you witness miracles of your own as you build your family.

MONEY
Just How Broke Are We Going to Be?

The $190,000 Myth

Money is one of the first topics raised when people discuss having more children, and for good reason: according to a calculation at Bankrate.com, it will cost you $190,000 to raise a child born in 2006 to age eighteen. Multiply that number by the ten children that my husband and I have, and you get the intimidating figure of nearly $2 million to raise our children to adulthood. No wonder people assume my husband must be King Midas.

I've seen estimates like that tossed around for years and wondered if they could possibly be true. Recently I decided to compare those averages to the costs at my house. The chart to the right shows the Bankrate numbers next to ours, broken down into categories. Remember, these are numbers per child. Later in the chapter, I'll talk about each category and how we keep things affordable at our house.

Large-Family Economics

This almost $52,000 total per child is much less intimidating than the "expert" estimate of $190,000. And this doesn't even fully factor in the diminishing cost of each subsequent child in a large family. Baby strollers, cribs, high chairs, and bunk beds can all be used again. Bikes

EXPENSE	BANKRATE.COM (Per Child)	MY FAMILY (Per Child)
Groceries	$1,525 per year	$840 per year
Clothing	$606 per year	$200 per year
Gift giving	$330 per year	$200 per year
Bigger home	$2,900 per year	$900 per year
Bigger car	$1,250 per year (ages 5 to 18)	$139 per year
Education	$600 per year (ages 5 to 18)	$100 per year (ages 5 to 18)
Recreation	$330 per year	$150 per year
Childcare	$4,300 per year (ages 0 to 11)	$20 per year (ages 0 to 11)
Additional insurance	$300 per year	$75 per year
Health care	$300 per year	$200 per year
Miscellaneous	$330 per year	$100 per year
TOTALS **1 child for 1 year** **1 child for 18 years**	$10,565 $190,528	$2,888 $51,984

and skates usually hold up for at least a couple of kids. Tonka trucks and Legos last forever.

Most families have two cars these days, no matter the size of the family. A minivan that works for two kids will also fit five. Yes, you'll eventually need a bigger house and a bigger vehicle if you want a really big family. But there's no need to call the real estate agent or start cruising car lots every single time you give birth.

Most items of clothing can last two or three kids. And the more children you have, the more likely people are to think of you when they have a bag of hand-me-downs to give away. We don't keep every item we're given. I like my kids to look up-to-date and neat, and some things we get are worn and out of style. But in any bag of hand-me-downs, there are usually at least a few really nice things that would be great additions to any child's wardrobe.

We usually buy new shoes, except in the case of Sunday shoes or when we find like-new Nikes at yard sales for three bucks. But between after-Thanksgiving sales and Payless, even shoes for ten don't have to empty dad's wallet.

Granted, the numbers for a family as big as mine still sound staggering. Raising ten kids will cost us half a million dollars even on Mary's Economy Plan. But when you divide that by eighteen years of child rearing, it's only $29,000 per year.

And remember: most really large families don't have the whole clan at home at once. My husband and I had a decade of parenting four or fewer kids at the beginning, and one year with eight children before our oldest went off to college. We currently have nine at home. But this fall, when our second child heads off to college, we'll be down to eight, and five years from now we'll probably have only six. With a little frugality, a large family can be totally manageable, even on a moderate income.

Frugality?

Is frugality a bad word to you? It terrifies some people. They associate it with trailer parks and rusty cars and housedresses and beans five days a week. They picture old ladies knotting soap slivers in old panty hose. They picture never eating out again. They picture deprivation.

Here's what I associate with frugality. I think of the privilege of being home with our children full time since 1998. I think of having every debt paid off except our house. I think of money in savings for

With a little frugality, a large family can be totally manageable, even on a moderate income. To me, frugality is not deprivation. Frugality is freedom.

emergencies. I think of being able to pay for Christmas via savings instead of Visa.

I love the sense of accomplishment I feel when I'm able to produce appealing, delicious food for $800 a month—and learning to cook Korean, Ethiopian, and Mexican food in the process. I think of taking our children to the Olympics, of visiting the ocean every year, of going camping every month all summer. I think of having the house paid off by the time we're fifty.

There's something even more miraculous we've been able to do, thanks in part to frugality. We've had the awesome privilege of bringing six children into our family through adoption. At around $15,000 per adoption, that is no small accomplishment. It is a testimony to God's providence that we've been able to do that on a moderate income. Those precious kids enrich our family more in one week than a brigade of BMWs or a million meals at Chili's.

To me, frugality is not deprivation. Frugality is freedom. Frugality gives us options. Yes, spending money with abandon allows us quick temporary pleasure: a meal out, a new pair of shoes, a manicure, or a trip to the movies. I'm not immune. I have nights when a 5 p.m. foray into the freezer produces nothing but brain freeze, and suddenly Pizza Hut sounds like my best friend. I buy clothes for children whose dresser drawers won't shut, and my Amazon.com obsession bends bookshelves all over my house.

Done occasionally, Happy Meals and Harlequins and even Hyundais aren't budget wreckers. Done habitually, purchases like this add up and have the potential to take away our big choices in life. Soon, instead of working because we find it fulfilling, we're working because we have two car payments and a keeping-up-with-my-sister house and enough credit card debt that we're popping Tylenol PM just to shut off our brains at bedtime.

What looked like freedom is really bondage, a forced march tied to a money-guzzling militant named Debt, all to pay for the stuff we impulsively bought last month or last year or two years ago. Gone is the freedom to make meaningful choices for our future or our children's.

Is there any way to turn it around? You bet.

A decade ago we had two jobs and two car payments and two credit cards' worth of debt. When we'd first gotten married, we honestly thought it would be a great thing for us both to be working parents. We imagined new cars, brand-name clothes, fancy vacations, and ballet lessons for our little girls.

But the more children we had, the harder it got emotionally for both of us to be working. The ballet class didn't balance out the babysitter like we'd imagined as newlyweds. Because we worked opposite shifts, we never had time for a date, let alone a weekend getaway. I cut back and cut back my shifts at the hospital, trying to find a more comfortable balance. By the time I gave birth to our fourth child, I was only working one or two days a week, usually on my husband's days off.

There were a dozen reasons this should have been a perfect compromise. I was well paid. Thanks to opposite shifts and doting grandmas, we rarely needed child care. I loved helping women breathe their way through labor and bathing their newborns and helping them breastfeed for the first time ever.

And yet I'd call home while I was at work and hear my baby cry over the phone and want to cry myself. Conveniently forgetting that the baby cried on my watch too, I'd growl at my husband to go take proper care of the baby. Then I'd hang up, stewing, and go use my breast pump in the bathroom and watch the clock creep until finally it was time to speed home and be reunited with my family. Once I got home, I was so tired from the long shift at work that I'd either snap at my hubby over the Lego bomb that had exploded in the living room or collapse into bed, craving sleep.

I thought more and more about quitting. My income wasn't enormous, but it covered groceries. Could we get by just on my husband's income? I read every book written about frugality in the past thirty years. I pulled out my folks' *Mother Earth News* magazines from their hippie days in the 1970s and '80s. I subscribed to the *Tightwad Gazette.* And I prayed.

When our fifth child came along, we decided to try the one-income thing, just for awhile. It actually worked. It worked so well that we've had five more children since then and I'm still home. We're not rich. But we are paying our bills and giving our kids what they need and loving our lives in the process. The rest of this chapter explains how we do it.

If you're looking to trim your budget, the easiest place to begin is at the grocery store. Most people can trim their grocery spending by a couple of hundred dollars per month . . .

Food

Groceries: If you're looking to trim your budget, the easiest place to begin is at the grocery store. Most people can trim their grocery spending by a couple of hundred dollars per month by implementing just two or three of the following suggestions. Doing all these things, I can feed my family on $800 per month.

Cook Most Food from Scratch: This doesn't involve endless slaving in the kitchen. I have at least half a dozen meals that I can get to the table in twenty minutes or less, and many others that take small amounts of prep time with a little longer cooking time. I keep a stash of convenience food for days I'm too busy to cook. Hot dogs, fish sticks, and good old peanut butter sandwiches make appearances at our house a few times a month each. But, in general, we eat home-cooked food. I especially love cooking Korean, Ethiopian, and Mexican food. Ethnic food tends to be healthy and affordable, not to mention delicious.

Plan Menus to Minimize Extra Trips to the Store: Every trip to the store is another opportunity for impulse buying. I go on grocery-shopping trips just twice a month. I've made a list of two-dozen dinners that we eat frequently, and I make sure to stock up on those ingredients. I don't specify which meal I'll serve each day. I like the freedom to choose what I want to cook. Of course I still forget things and make extra trips now and then. Sometimes the cats eat dog food for a day, or we go a few days without bananas. But a two-week menu plan dramatically reduces the number of times I hit Wal-Mart and makes me much more able to resist the urge to eat out.

Watch Prices and Buy Food Where It Is Cheapest: Like anyone, I'm tempted to buy things where they are most convenient. Wal-Mart is my friend, especially for the odds and ends I need between the big shopping trips. But for my big twice-monthly trips, I visit the most affordable stores, which in my area is WinCo for most things and Costco for a few others.

Grow a Garden and Preserve the Extra Produce: Not everyone has the space or the inclination for a big garden. But if you do, you'll improve your family's diet and decrease your grocery bill. Our garden probably saves us $100 a month on groceries, year-round. Even a couple of tomato plants in barrels on your patio can save you money; from there you can branch out if you are inclined. Don't forget that when you have a big family, you also have many hands to help with the gardening. About three mornings a week in the summertime, my whole family spends half an hour in the garden, weeding and watering. Little ones start helping around age five, as soon as they can tell tomatoes from weeds. By the time they're eight or nine, they are real contributors.

Buy on Sale and Stock Up: When corn flakes are a buck a box, I'll buy 8 boxes. If hamburger or chicken breasts are $1.50 a pound or less, I'll buy ten meals worth. It is not uncommon for me to walk out of the grocery store with fifty pounds of burger in my basket. As you might guess, a freezer is an important part of my budget, and remember, if your pantry space is limited, there's nothing wrong with creative storage. You may discover that the perfect place for that extra cereal is under your bed. Just don't forget it's there!

Treat Meat as a Condiment Instead of the Centerpiece: We eat meat in moderation. Our spaghetti is heavy on tomatoes, onions, garlic, and mushrooms, but contains only a pound or two of hamburger for all twelve of us. My kung pao chicken features four types of vegetables stir-fried with garlic, red pepper, and sesame oil, but it only requires five chicken breasts. This approach to eating meat is both affordable and healthy.

Eat Out in Moderation: A great thing about planning meals ahead of time is that a full pantry makes it easier to resist the lure of fast food. If you have the ingredients for your own kung pao chicken in the fridge, the nearest Speedy Panda is much less tempting. When we do eat out, we look for large-family-friendly specials, like the Pizza Hut deal where you can buy a medium pizza for $6.

*When bargain shopping can be seen as a game of skill
instead of a necessary evil, it encourages contentment
and helps kids be better stewards of their money.*

Clothing

Like any mom, I love seeing my children in beautiful clothes. But it isn't necessary to go into debt to keep children looking stylish and well clothed. Hand-me-downs are a great resource for many large families. Thrift shops, consignment stores, eBay, and end-of-season clearances are also good places to find affordable clothing. I visit yard sales at least two or three times each summer, keeping an eye out for anything I'll need in the next year or so.

I stock up on jeans and socks at after-Thanksgiving sales. I pass down our clothes from child to child. We're also blessed to have a grandma who loves to buy our children clothes for birthdays and Christmas.

By the time children get old enough to want specific brands of jeans or shoes, they're also old enough to earn money of their own. But a funny thing happens when kids are in charge of buying their own extras. Their gotta-have-it list tends to get considerably shorter, and they become much more interested in prices.

All our kids enjoy visiting yard sales with me each summer. They've learned the joys of bargain shopping. One of my sons once bought a huge set of Hot Wheels for a dollar. Another son bought an apple box full of baseball cards for $20, then proceeded to sell the half of them that he didn't want on eBay for $50. My teenaged daughters love watching friends' jaws drop when they learn you can buy perfect $60 name-brand jeans at yard sales for $5. When bargain shopping can be seen as a game of skill instead of a necessary evil, it encourages contentment and helps kids be better stewards of their money.

Gift Giving

When children are invited to other kids' birthday parties, we give simple gifts such as craft supplies, a favorite book, or homemade play dough. Since our children are homeschooled, we avoid some of the party craziness. On an average, they are invited to just a couple of good friends' parties each year.

At Christmastime I shop early and thoughtfully. Little children's wishes are simple. One-year-olds are very content to open two or three well-chosen gifts and then settle in to play, usually with the paper and ribbons. Five-year-olds don't care how much you've spent as long as the gift is well chosen. Soon enough they will be teenagers and their wishes will be more expensive, so keep it simple as long as you can.

We allow our children to write a variety of Christmas gift ideas (both large and small) on a list on the fridge. If a computer or a pony finds its way onto the list, I don't hesitate to tell a child that item is something to save their money for.

Housing

We have been blessed when it comes to housing. Our first house was a fixer-upper. Four years and three kids later, when we needed a bigger home, the sweat equity we'd put into it paid off big time: we sold the house for twice the price. That was our nest egg for our current home, which we built ourselves. Though not a palace, it has nearly 3,000 square feet and six bedrooms. We added three of the six bedrooms after we moved into the house. Sweat equity has maximized the value of our home without overextending our budget.

Not all people can do handyman work to increase the equity—or the square footage—in their homes. But think carefully about your needs before you overbuy. Sometimes I fantasize about a bigger house, but the thought of the king's-ransom mortgage payments quickly makes me thankful for what we have.

Vehicles

Vehicle expenses vary tremendously from family to family. Some families feel that a new vehicle every year or two is essential to their happiness. We are content with a vehicle as long as it is reliable and works for our purposes. Like most people, we had car payments for quite a few years. When we paid off that last car loan a few years back, wow, did we ever feel free.

Sure, we pay for repairs now and then. But the occasional $600 repair bill is better than paying $300 every single month for years.

We paid $20,000 for our current fifteen-passenger van when it was one year old. We're hoping it will last throughout the largest years of our family. Already our oldest is off at college, and the van is still going strong. Hopefully, by the time it needs to be replaced, our family will have shrunk enough to fit into a more affordable used minivan. Though we've bought several cars that were only a year old, I doubt we'll ever buy a brand-new car because of that initial depreciation cost.

Education

The cost of different educational choices varies widely. Families who send their kids to private school will obviously have the highest education costs. Homeschooling is a very affordable option for large families like mine. A $50 algebra textbook is a bargain when used by ten children, ditto for learning games and reading books. Even a frog dissection kit can be used again—though you'll need a new frog each year!

We borrow books from the library, four or five dozen at a time. In August, when school supplies are on sale, we buy notebooks and pencils by the dozen. We've been the happy recipients of at least three only slightly outdated computers from my computer-geek brothers, as well as a perfectly functional copy machine. A good place to check for schoolbooks is eBay. Yard sales are also great sources, especially for readers for younger children.

Insurance/Medical

Medical care can be expensive. But many employers don't charge any more to insure a family of ten than they do a family of three. The family insurance plan at my husband's work charges $50 extra per month to cover the entire family, no matter how big. We have excellent preventative health and dental insurance, and our maximum out-of-pocket each year is only $2,000. We also benefit from a medical savings plan that ensures we have at least enough money set aside for an average year of medical needs.

When thinking about the cost of medical care, I was struck by the different ways that God provides. My parents raised eight children on a pastor's salary with minimal health insurance. God provided for them by simply keeping us healthy. In two decades my folks faced one tonsillectomy and three broken bones.

When John and I were young college students, my obstetric care was given to us as a gift by my mom's employer, who was an obstetrician. We currently have a son whose $12,000 prosthetic leg has to be replaced each year. Our expenses are high, but God is providing for us once again, this time with excellent medical insurance through my husband's employer.

Child Care

I am guessing that our estimate of $20 per year per child for babysitting looked a little ridiculous to some. I am quick to admit that we have a nearly ideal situation. During the decade that I was employed as a nurse, I worked mostly on my husband's days off. Relatives provided most of the additional child care we needed before we had capable teenagers. During those first twelve years of parenting, before our oldest kids were able to babysit, we paid a babysitter maybe three times a year.

In my estimates at the beginning of this chapter, I rounded that to $20 per child per year for the first eleven years. But, in reality, that was only an expense for the older children. Some families may choose to go out on dates more often than we do. Others may have teens who are too busy to babysit, and, obviously, many families need daily child care while both parents work. But my purpose in sharing our (very low) numbers is to encourage others to think of ways they could make budget changes if they choose to.

Activities/Enrichment

Our children participate in one or two extracurricular activities per year each, such as baseball, swimming, soccer, piano, and choir. In general, we do not begin extra-curricular activities that cost money until our children are eight or so. The higher cost of teenager's activities is offset by the low- or no-cost things we do with our younger ones, which makes $150 a year per child adequate. I'll talk more about children and activities in the fourth chapter.

Low-cost activities include occasional trips to the dollar theaters for movies and visits to the water park on the free day sponsored by my husband's work. We camp at state parks or at Grandma's place in the mountains. Fun does not have to break the bank or involve large black mouse ears. We've told our kids (only half-jokingly) that Disneyland is a great place for a honeymoon. They're fine with it. So are we.

On the other hand, a trip to the ocean once or twice a year is essential in our book. This spring, for the third year in a row, we rented a great beach house. Off-season, it is a mere $900 for a week. Not bad for twelve people. That includes four bedrooms, two bathrooms, and an ocean view. Ah, bliss.

To our family, the beach beats Disneyland any day. Other families consider Disneyland a childhood essential. The important thing to realize is that most budgets won't fit everything. Think hard about what adds the most quality of life for your family. Spending thoughtfully helps you feel more satisfied with the shape of your life.

Think hard about what adds the most quality of life for
your family. Spending thoughtfully helps you feel more
satisfied with the shape of your life.

College

Many people assume that about the time that pink line shows up on
the pregnancy test, responsible parents also start a college savings
account. That's a fine idea, if you feel called to do it and are able to do
so. But John and I don't consider that a set-in-concrete responsibility
of parents. In fact, we passionately believe that kids learn extremely
important things by being responsible for their own college educations.

We were fortunate to be able to get through college with very little
help from either set of parents. We worked hard, got some financial aid,
took out a few loans, and made it through. Sure, we paid on those loans
for a few years. But we also graduated with skills that made the job
hunt easy once we graduated. During our college years, we saw many
people flunk out of school on Daddy's money. People value money more
if they make it themselves. We have confidence that if our children want
to go to school badly enough, they'll find a way to make it through.

Of course we'll be there to back our kids if they get in a jam.
Budgeting during those first years away from home can be tough, and
we may have to extend a no-interest loan now and then. But if our
kids see school as their own responsibility, we think they will work
harder at it.

We also believe that college is not the only path to success in life.
There are dozens of perfectly good careers with no college requirement.
A skilled electrician with zero college can make more than the average
teacher with a college degree. I personally know quite a few people

who never found their college degrees useful. So we are definitely not pushing college as a one-size-fits-all solution for our kids.

As homeschooling parents, we are contributing to our children's future success by providing the best high school education possible, focusing on areas that interest them most. We've taught them the value of hard work, and we are teaching them how to find answers to questions themselves.

We're doing our best to encourage our children along paths that interest them. For some children that has meant architecture books and computer-aided design programs. For others it has meant boatloads of classic literature, piano lessons, or advanced math books. Still, others have requested computer-programming books so advanced and so thick that a yawn forms in my throat when I look at the title. The kids who are interested enough to plow through those things will doubtless be my computer gurus in a few years.

We've paid for test prep books so that when kids take the SAT and the ACT, they'll be equipped to score as high as possible and hopefully be eligible for scholarships. Our oldest daughter was able to do just that. With a combination of four different scholarships and some Pell Grants, her first year of college was completely paid, right down to housing, food, books, and gas money.

Students from large families often qualify for need-based grant money. Some people might say that's freeloading on the basis of family size. I remember all the years we've been homeschooling while paying public school taxes, and figure we're finally getting back a little of that money.

Don't get me wrong—I'm not saying that people who feel strongly about paying for their children's college shouldn't do it. Different families are called in different directions, and certainly not all adult children squander the gift of a free education. But I don't believe the presence or absence of a college fund should be a reason to have or not to have more children. Kids can get through school without being fully funded by their folks.

I don't believe the presence or absence of a college fund should be a reason to have or not to have more children. Kids can get through school without being fully funded by their folks.

What Do Children Really Need?

Making it work on a moderate income comes down to clarity of purpose. What do our children need most from us? They need love. They need food, clothes, and shelter. They need clear expectations and responsibilities. They need time just to be kids. They need faith in a power higher than themselves. But they do not need huge allowances, rooms of their own, TVs in their rooms, and name-brand clothes.

If the dream of your heart is to have a larger family, find agreement with your spouse and then go forward with confidence. Most budgets will cover children's needs just fine. The trick is to make wise decisions about the wants.

During our parenting journey, I have been amazed at the providence we've experienced. We've been blessed with $50 health insurance, $3 Nikes, on-sale winter coats, half-price jeans, free rollerblades, and full-ride college scholarships. We've even been given a couple of vehicles.

If you're considering adding to your family, don't worry about the grocery bills or the cost of Little League or the number of bedrooms in your house. Kids grow fine sharing rooms, and God does fine at stretching budgets. In fact, I suspect he takes delight in surprising us with just how well he can provide.

MAKING SPACE

Will We Need a Shoehorn
to Fit Another Bed?

Over the years, when John and I have begun talking about adding
another child to our family, it always makes us take a critical look at our
house. Suddenly, all we can see is the bulging toy box, the Little Tikes
table in the entryway, and the mountain of laundry that seems to be a
permanent fixture in front of the washer. There have been times when
a first glance around the house made us wonder if we could even fit
another child.

Even couples expecting a first or second baby will find themselves
in the throes of the third-trimester panic, dismantling a home office or
selling a treadmill or thinking that the garage would be better utilized
as a rec room. That time of expectancy is a great time to reevaluate
your space. But an addition to the family does not always warrant an
addition to the house.

Living in the Western world gives people a skewed perspective about
the amount of space needed to raise a family. It is easy to look at the
subdivisions with triple-car garages and to notice that our friends'
kids all have their own rooms and to start thinking that much space is
essential. But families have been thriving for centuries on far less space
than we consider normal today.

When my grandmother was raising kids in the 1950s, many families
lived in two-bedroom, one-bathroom houses that were no more than

Living in the Western world gives
people a skewed perspective about the
amount of space needed to raise a family.

1,200 square feet. Back then, most families had four or five kids. Young children shared a bedroom for several years. When it was time to divide the boys from the girls, a porch would often be enclosed and turned into a sleeping area for the boys.

For an even more recent perspective, you only have to visit another country. All over the world today, people live in spaces that Americans would consider unacceptable. In Ethiopia, whole families of eight or ten people routinely live in one-room shacks. Ideal? Of course not. But it works.

This type of space efficiency is not limited to third-world countries. When we visited ultra-modern Seoul in 2000 to adopt one of our sons, we visited his foster mom's apartment. It consisted of a main room of perhaps fifteen by eighteen feet, two bedrooms no larger than nine by ten each, and a small bathroom. Three adults and four children lived in this space of no more than 600 square feet.

Even now in ultra-expensive places like New York City, families of four will live in one-bedroom apartments with a Murphy bed or a hide-a-bed couch turning the living room into a second bedroom at night.

Some large families are fortunate enough to have almost unlimited living space. But a huge house is not essential. And most growing families will benefit from making their home work smarter, whether they are a mega family in the 'burbs or a family of five squeezing into an apartment in New York City.

If your 2,000-square-foot house is costing you $1,500 per month, you're paying $9 a year for every single square foot in your house.

De-Clutter

Start by hunting around your home for the things you rarely use. You may feel less sentimental about those ancient *National Geographic* magazines or the dusty stuffed animals if you take a few moments to calculate how many dollars you pay each year for each square foot of space in your home. If your 2,000-square-foot house is costing you $1,500 per month, you're paying $9 a year for every single square foot in your house. Giving away what you don't use will allow you to better use your space and benefit the people to whom you give your unused items.

Last year, after our ninth and tenth children came home, we realized that we could really use a sixth bedroom in our home. My first thought was an expensive bumpout. After I priced a single-bedroom addition at $20,000 for materials alone, I was inspired to take a more creative look at our house.

Our large upstairs family room looked full at first glance, but it was full of things we rarely used. We got rid of a treadmill, an ancient couch, a couple of shelves, and a gargantuan desk. We pared down our book collection, tossed out old magazines, and organized toys.

A couple of days working freed one whole corner of the family room, which we walled off and turned into a small but beautifully functional sixth bedroom. Total cost: $1,000, including a new window and bunk beds. The family room still fits a piano, a foosball table, a library, and a computer corner, but it now houses a new bedroom as well. The kids are thrilled with their space, and I am thrilled with the affordability of the "addition."

Rooms in Your Home

Living Rooms: Some areas of the home take only minor tweaking to handle more people. Living room seating can easily be expanded with beanbag chairs that are kept in children's bedrooms and gotten out when you're planning a family movie evening. If your living room is big enough to handle it, an L-shaped couch unit gives a lot of seating for the square footage it takes.

If you know a handyman, an even more space-conscious choice is an L-shaped bench built right into two walls of the living room and then made comfortable with good-quality cushions. Build some storage underneath the benches for toys or books. You might also add a combination ottoman/coffee table to put your feet up on. I have recently seen beautiful examples of this type of built-in seating in upscale home-design magazines.

When you're shopping for living room furniture, look for durable fabric and don't skip the stain guard. Some moms swear by easy-wash slipcovers, but I find they take a lot of fluffing and retucking to stay neat. I much prefer just choosing a couch made from durable material. Double-sided couch cushions are a huge plus, since accidental damage to a cushion can be hidden by simply flipping over the cushion.

Many moms of large families swear by leather furniture. We took the plunge and bought two leather couches about four years ago. I love them. They wipe clean easily and so far seem very durable. I would suggest a fairly dark color to more easily hide the occasional ink pen mark. Of course in an ideal world, two-year-olds wouldn't run around wielding ink pens, but that isn't the world I happen to inhabit. Recently, I was even able to remove a blop of nail polish from a couch cushion, much to the relief of the culprits.

Dining Rooms: Dining room seating can be expanded by replacing some of your chairs with benches. In fact, if you anticipate needing more seating in the future and are in the market for a dining set, go ahead and buy benches to start with. Benches have a nice streamlined look to them, fit more kids in the same amount of space, and are much easier to clean than chairs.

If your table is in a corner of the dining room, think about buying or custom-building an L-shaped bench to wrap around two sides of the table for maximum space efficiency. Kids have no trouble climbing in and out of bench seating. Keep at least a few standard chairs for the comfort of adults.

When it comes to high chairs, many families these days are opting for small booster-type seats that strap onto a regular chair at the table, instead of the freestanding kind that take up so much storage space when the baby is not using it. These little seats are also much easier to tote to Grandma's.

Laundry Rooms: The laundry room can get out of control quickly as a family grows. Some families give their bigger kids assigned days of the week on which to do their own laundry. Other families opt to buy double washers and dryers. After the addition of our ninth and tenth children last year, I was sorely tempted to go that route. Instead, we bought a front-loading washer—a Whirlpool Duet.

This washer is a dream. Not only does it use less water, it also spins clothes so dry that our dryer gets done twice as fast. In the past I'd have to turn the dryer on two or three times before the clothes got dry. Now one cycle is enough, which means the laundry gets done so much more efficiently. I should have bought this washer years ago!

I've also developed a system of laundry management. Next to my washer, I have a shelf containing two baskets for dirty laundry. Across the room from our washer and dryer, instead of the traditional lower cabinets, we've installed a couple of long shelves. Each shelf is long enough to accommodate three full-sized laundry baskets into which I sort the clean laundry. I've assigned one basket to each of our six bedrooms. Next to the dryer we have a huge basket designated for linens and towels and another for socks.

When a load of laundry is dry, we immediately sort everything straight from the dryer into the appropriate baskets. We also have a long closet rod mounted right near the ceiling, spanning the length of the laundry room for things that need to be hung up or that can't go into the dryer.

Every Wednesday and Saturday, people collect their baskets and fold and put away their own clothing. My elementary-aged kids fold towels and sheets along with their own clothing. The teenagers help the under-fives with their clothing, gradually training them to fold their own laundry and also helping them put it away properly.

The sort-into-baskets method works well for me. I am usually in too much of a hurry to fold and put away everything right out of the dryer, but I usually have enough time to at least sort things into baskets. Once things make it into baskets, people can easily locate a favorite shirt or a missing swimsuit even if the laundry hasn't been put away for awhile.

I am fortunate to have a good-sized laundry room. But even if your laundry room consists only of a large closet, you could probably custom-build shelving over the washer and dryer to house laundry baskets that would allow you to sort laundry straight from the dryer.

Bathrooms: The bathroom is another place that can be strained by large numbers of children. My dream home would have a Jack and Jill bathroom between each pair of children's bedrooms. Each bedroom would have its own sink area, separated from the toilet/shower area by doors.

We don't have Jack and Jill bathrooms, but we have been able to add toothbrush sinks on both levels of our home. The downstairs bathroom is right across the hall from the laundry room. Recently, we replaced our ugly plastic laundry sink with a deep stainless steel sink set into a low counter. We put a mirror above the sink and mounted a custom cup holder on the wall with a spot for every child's cup and toothbrush. The sink is still big enough to soak a stained shirt or to wash out a paint roller when we need to. But it also works well as a tooth-brushing sink in the evenings, when multiple children are brushing teeth and using the toilet before heading off to bed. This has really cut down on the arguing at bedtime.

When we added a sixth bedroom last year, we came up with a similar fix for the upstairs bathroom. We have a small corner just outside the bathroom that we realized was just big enough for a small vanity, mirror, and sink. Now the kids who live upstairs can get to their toothbrushes or take out contacts at bedtime even if someone is showering or using the bathroom.

If you don't have a place in your house for another sink, equip each bedroom with a mirror and grooming supplies. This way kids can at least comb their hair and put on makeup in the bedroom instead of always needing to do these things in the bathroom.

In the old days, bedrooms were routinely outfitted with a pitcher and basin for washing up in the morning and at bedtime. This might be a charming way to ease the bathroom crunch, especially if you have a teenaged daughter who you know will be careful with water in the bedroom. Sometimes you don't need a bigger house. You just need to think of creative ways to better use what you already have.

Bedrooms: Although bedroom sharing is the norm in many parts of the world, many people in America these days see one child per bedroom as ideal. Some large families have that luxury. But most families will end up with at least some of their kids sharing rooms. If that is your situation, don't feel guilty or apologetic. Kids who share rooms during childhood are learning all sorts of useful life lessons. They are better prepared for the give and take of room sharing as adults when they get

> Kids who share rooms during childhood are
> learning all sorts of useful life lessons.

married. They also have a chance to develop sibling relationships in a
way that is not possible when kids hole up in separate sanctuaries all
over the house.

Briana, a mother of two, says she shared a room with her sister
while growing up:

> *I think it created a bond between us. Those late nights giggling
> and turning on our flashlights to sneak in a game of cards
> after bedtime were a special time. During the school year, we
> had our twin beds across the room from each other but got
> to push them together in the middle of the room during the
> summer. I always looked forward to that.*

Jen, a mother of two young children, also noticed that room sharing
helped her children's relationships with each other:

> *When our oldest was one, my husband started medical school.
> He took a huge pay cut, and we moved to one of the most
> expensive housing markets in the country. Little money =
> little house. We had two bedrooms. Our second child was
> born while we lived there. He moved into the bedroom with
> his sister when he was ready, and that is where the best little
> friendship ever began. From their first nights together they
> would lay in their room and talk and play (very quietly). And
> when Little Man got a bit older, we would sometimes even
> find that he had crawled out of his toddler bed and into Big*

Sister's bed to sleep. It was not something we planned or
even considered ideal in the beginning, but the kids sharing
a bedroom was a true blessing! Now that we have four
bedrooms, they still sleep in the same bedroom all the time.

Functional Bedrooms: When you're setting up a small- to medium-sized bedroom for two or more children, be selective about what is stored there. Some families opt to keep most of the toys in a different room. Exceptions might be a stuffed animal or two and a small treasure bin for each child.

Another way to reduce clutter is to pare down kids' wardrobes. If a child only has six or eight outfits, there's only so much mess he can make, even if he does pull everything out of his drawers at once. Most large families wash laundry so often that it's not a big deal to cycle the clothing through fast enough to be worn again when the drawer gets empty.

My boys wouldn't bat an eye at this approach. They tend to wear the same four shirts until I'm ready to burn them anyway. But my girls would protest at such limited wardrobe options, and, frankly, I love having a variety of clothing for my children to wear as well. Still, I try to keep clothing quantities reasonable. No kid really needs two dozen shirts, and passing on what you don't need to others will make your life easier and will benefit the people to whom you give the extra clothing.

One creative way to deal with clothing clutter is to store all the children's clothing in the laundry room. It sounds a little unconventional, but it is another perfect example of thinking creatively. You can keep the clothes in baskets on shelves, or build cubbies for each child that look something like school lockers with hanging space above and shelving below. One mom pulled all the cabinets out of one side of her laundry room. She then moved four dressers into the space, lined them up side by side, and hung all the hang-up clothing on a long rod above the dressers.

One creative way to deal with clothing
clutter is to store all the children's
clothing in the laundry room.

This totally removes the clothing clutter from kids' rooms and makes it much simpler to put away laundry. Kids go into the laundry room every morning to pick out their clothing. Any mom who has walked into her four-year-old daughter's room to discover the whole dresser emptied onto the floor will see the benefit of keeping the clothing somewhere other than in the bedroom.

There are lots of ways to make bedrooms more efficient for two or more children. You can find some really nice custom-made triple bunk beds for sale. For ideas, check out http://www.wayoutwood.com/ or http://www.bunkloft.com/. When we had three girls sharing one room for awhile, my husband built an L-shaped loft for the bigger girls. This allowed us to tuck the dressers under the loft beds, freeing floor space for a third bed.

One mom raising four girls in New York City found a creative way to make a two-bedroom apartment work for her family. She had two sets of bunk beds made with a thin wall between them. Under the lower bunks were drawers, and at the foot of each bed was a dresser. Built into the headboard of each bed was a bookshelf and a reading light. This custom quad bunk gave each child a bit of privacy, even though the room was home to four children.

Another family wanted to fit two kids into a very small bedroom of about nine by ten while still leaving floor space to play. They took the doors off the closet and built a custom bunk bed right in the closet. The bunks were wider than the depth of the closet, so they protruded from the closet a foot or so. But the combination of under-bed drawers and a large freestanding wardrobe allowed adequate storage while still giving the children a good amount of floor space.

Speaking of clothes, most moms of large families opt to save at least some of their older children's clothing for younger ones. For years I filled the top shelves of kids' closets with outgrown clothes. Recently I reclaimed that closet space by moving outgrown and off-season clothing to the garage. I installed shelving high on the wall in our garage and sorted all the clothing into labeled plastic bins. Every time I am out there now I get a twinge of pleasure to see all those bins lined up and labeled, and to know that I can easily find what I need when I need it.

Over years of toy buying and toy receiving and toy sorting and toy tossing, I've come to realize that there really are only a few good toys.

Toys

Toy storage can be a huge issue for large families. Awhile ago, I was at Toys R Us doing some Christmas shopping. Even without my kids in tow, I must have had that frazzled-mom look, because I was approached by a woman in a business suit who asked for advice. She was shopping for her nephew's second birthday and was debating between an electronic learning toy and a stuffed animal. Which did I recommend?

Thinking of the bins of mostly unused stuffed animals at home, I advised her emphatically away from the teddy bear. The woman looked crestfallen. It was obvious that the teddy bear was calling to her—and no wonder. They're cute and cuddly and seem like the perfect gift. But most American kids over the age of six months have enough stuffed plush to stock a toy store, and they don't play with half of them.

Over years of toy buying and toy receiving and toy sorting and toy tossing, I've come to realize that there really are only a few good toys. If your space is at a premium, you may as well invest in toys with staying power.

Legos: Small Legos are great for older kids, and they're very space efficient, especially if you combine two or three sets into one big bin. The down side of Legos is that they aren't safe for babies. It can be a pain for the older kids to have to pick up their Legos every time the baby comes into the room. A great compromise is Duplo Legos. They're big enough to be safe for little ones, and the extra size makes it possible to create impressive-looking structures. Even my husband and my ten-year-olds enjoy playing Duplos with the younger children. We have a huge bin of them that we've compiled from lots of sets over the years, and when family asks what a child needs for a birthday or Christmas, I will often suggest an addition to the set.

Dollhouses: Every family with little ones should have some kind of a dollhouse. Playmobile and Fisher-Price are my favorites for fun accessories and durability. Even little boys will play with dollhouses if there are plenty of cars for the "vroom" factor, and maybe even some cool-looking firefighters or construction workers.

Play Dishes and Food: Our play dishes have been collected from many sets over the years and fill a small plastic bin. Many people like to buy kids those huge plastic play kitchens to go along with the dishes. They're cute, but I'd rather not have something that takes so much space. Kids can have just as much fun spreading out the dishes on a shelf or small table. In warm weather, try drawing a stove in chalk on the front steps, and give your child a basin of water for dishwashing. If it's too cold to play with water outdoors, you can spread a couple of bath towels on the floor and give the kids real water, sugar, and saltines for an indoor tea party. Ah, bliss.

Dress-Up Boxes: One Christmas I told the grandmothers and aunties in our family that we were putting together a dress-up box for our little girls, and asked for donations of old finery. They kindly contributed old high heels, scarves, hats, gloves, and costume jewelry. We added old dance costumes, lace curtains, and Halloween costumes to the mix and stored it all in a big bin. As our collection has grown over the years, I've had to buy bigger and bigger bins. Our current dress-up box would probably hold a Labrador retriever—it takes a fair bit of real estate. But it has been pulled out and played with at least once or twice a week for over a decade. In my mind, it is a great use of space.

Outdoor Toys: A good-quality wagon will last you for years and can double as a stroller when you take preschoolers for walks. We have a portable basketball hoop in our driveway that sees action every week. There's also a fun series of jumbo-sized games out these days. Monster Golf and Monster Tennis have both been hits with our kids. And every kid needs balls, sand-digging toys, and a bike.

Books, Books, Books

Every household should have a good collection of books. Narnia, Little House on the Prairie, Childhood of Famous Americans, Junie B. Jones, and almost anything by Beverly Cleary are proven winners. The library is a wonderful resource as well. But kids should be able to find something to read anytime, not just when you have time to hit the library.

Art Supplies

Art supplies make great gifts. They are creative, space-efficient, and when they're gone, you can throw them away and regain the space. You can never have too much paint, glitter, paper, scissors, markers, glue, collage supplies, and play dough!

Do you despise play dough? I used to hate it too. My kids love it, but I always ended up on my knees picking it out of the carpet afterwards. Then a fellow mom of many told me she only allows play dough outdoors on the picnic table. Cleanup involves simply sweeping crumbs into the grass. This idea totally changed my mind about play dough!

To keep your toys under control, you'll probably need to sort them out at least once or twice a year. Don't hesitate to give away the toys that are not being used. Remember, everything you own takes space. Make sure that everything occupying the real estate in your home is pulling its weight. You might just decide you'd rather have empty space in the corner of your family room instead of that child's easel that never gets used.

Durable Homes

Though I am a tightwad at heart, years of mothering a large family have made me a reluctant fan of high-quality components in certain places. A kitchen faucet in a home with several children gets turned on literally dozens of times every day. You don't have to buy the most expensive faucet out there, but you won't regret going high end. Steer clear of faucets with single levers that lift and lower and control both hot and cold. Kids will lean on those with a lot of body weight, and soon they will break and leak. We've found that faucets with separate levers for hot and cold, and pull-forward, push-back operating motion are most durable.

Other things that take tremendous abuse from large families include carpet, cabinets, kitchen flooring, and doorknobs. We've lived in our home since 1993 and have replaced the front door knob three times. We've learned to buy the more expensive ones because they hold up much better.

We paid top dollar for our living room carpet when we built the home, and I've never regretted it. It has been extremely durable. Most moms know to steer clear of extremely light-colored carpet. Brown

We paid top dollar for our living room
carpet when we built the home,
and I've never regretted it.

is practical but can be dull. If you want to go with a more interesting color, pick a carpet with a good bit of color variation between the strands, since that will hide stains better. We chose a variegated green carpet, and I have loved it.

Pergo-type floors can be problematic for growing families. The color doesn't go all the way through, so the first time a kid scuffs his way through the kitchen with rocks stuck in his baseball cleats, you'll have scratches. It is also sensitive to water damage, making it curl if not properly installed.

Many parents swear by wood floors for durability. The trick is to apply a durable finish and keep up with it so that any water leakage is repelled. When we added wood in our front entryway, I finished it with five coats of polyurethane. I joked I was putting on one coat per child. It took a long time to put that many coats on it, but five kids and ten years later, it is still going strong.

The color variation in the oak does an excellent job of hiding dirt, and the poly finish makes water simply bead up without damaging the wood. It has lost some of the high gloss that it had at first, and there are a few scratches, but it still looks beautiful and takes all the abuse our busy family can dish out.

We have yet to find a dishwasher that will last more than three years. When you consider we run two or three loads a day, I guess that's not too surprising. Our appliance salesperson told us that the average family washes four loads of dishes a week and gets seven or eight years out of their dishwasher. With a twinkle in her eye, she said we'd probably better guesstimate our dishwasher's "normal" life in dog years.

Creativity Is Key

Certainly all these ideas won't be right for your family and your home. But hopefully I've demonstrated some possibilities and gotten you thinking about ways you can improve the functionality of the home you have. With a little creative thinking, you will probably find a way to fit another child into your family without resorting to either a shoehorn or a budget-breaking remodeling project.

KIDS AND ACTIVITIES

Is It Still "Home Sweet Home" If I'm Never There?

A big part of childhood these days is the activities merry-go-round. If you already have a couple of kids, you know about the busyness that surrounds children and their activities. Between dance class and soccer and music lessons and play dates, kids spend many afternoons and evenings away from home. Is it possible for a mom to keep up with multiple children and their activities?

Money and time are indeed issues. Even the most organized people only have twenty-four hours in a day. Finances can only stretch so far, and mom's minivan can be in only one place at a time. Especially if you're raising half a dozen or more kids, you will probably find yourself making decisions about your children's activities with a more appraising eye. But it is completely possible for kids from large families to still have active involved lives.

Extracurricular Activities

When surveying the wonderful array of activities available to our children, it can be hard to sort out what is worthwhile and what isn't. Guilt plays a part as well. Should a kid have to skip swim team just because his sister is taking gymnastics across town at the same time? What if you're squelching Olympic-level talent?

Most parents who are committed to having a large family are prepared to make a few sacrifices themselves. But no one wants their kids to miss out on experiences just because of the number of children in the family. These decisions can be difficult and emotional, both for parents and for children. You may find more clarity in your decision making if you ask yourself some questions as you consider each activity.

What is the goal of this activity? Are you hoping to help your child become more physically active? Do you want your kids to get some socialization time with other children? Do you want to introduce them to a new sport? Get better at an activity they love? Gain a musical talent they can use for life?

What will your family gain from this activity? Does your family enjoy watching this activity? Will you all gain pleasure from hearing your young musician improve? Will the activity allow your family to spend time together?

What is the cost in both time and money? Along with the cost of the activity itself, will there be extra fees for uniforms, tournaments, and instruments? Don't forget the gas you will spend driving the child from place to place. Unless you're extremely organized, there will also most likely be extra meals eaten out if you're living in the car, driving kids from place to place around mealtime.

What will your family lose from participating in this activity? How will this new activity impact your family time? Experts agree that successful kids tend to come from families who eat together. How many dinners will your family miss out on because of this activity? What will mom sacrifice to make this happen? Perhaps her patience as she runs from place to place? Will younger siblings lose time to play as they spend their afternoons in mom's shuttle bus?

Experts agree that successful kids tend to come from families who eat together.

These questions are difficult but crucial to consider if you want to keep some control over the quality of your life. Once you have thought them through, you'll be able to more clearly weigh the advantages and disadvantages. Ask yourself if you could give your children these advantages at a lower cost to your family.

When our oldest kids were in elementary school, we jumped into sports with both feet—soccer for three, all at once, on different teams, on different fields, sometimes in different towns.

We enjoyed cheering our children on and watching them improve at a sport they enjoyed, but our family paid a price. We were eating fast food constantly. The preschoolers had every soccer field in town rated by the quality/presence of the nearby playground equipment. I had every soccer field in town rated by the quality and cleanliness of the bathrooms. And bedtime stories, a precious part of family life, took a two-month hiatus during soccer season. Thankfully, it was only for two months—we had the sense to sign up only for spring soccer. But our family definitely paid a price.

When our oldest soccer player turned thirteen, the intensity ratcheted up a notch. About a third of her games were out of town—far out of town—sometimes as far as two hours away. Between drive time, warm-up, and the actual game, one game could easily take half a day—and that was for a rec-league team. After a couple of seasons of juggling, we reluctantly decided that organized soccer was costing our family too much, and took some time off.

After a couple of years off, though, some of the kids were really hankering to play again. Thankfully around that time we learned that friends of ours were organizing a casual soccer game every Friday evening in the park. We have participated in this for a couple of years now, and it is great fun.

Anyone over age six or so is welcome to play, and in our group there are players of all abilities. Some truly excellent competitive-league soccer players show up every week just for the love of the game. There are younger ones who've never played organized soccer. Parents play too, if they're inclined. Rules are loose and corners of the field are sometimes marked with water bottles and sweatshirts. But the competition is fierce.

The kids who are too small to be safe on the field can play on the playground or kick balls around just for fun. Parents not involved in the "big" game chat while little kids play. About the time the little kids get tired of the playground, the big people come panting off the soccer field, rosy-cheeked and happy, and we all reluctantly head home.

Family soccer night has been a great compromise for us for a couple of years. We are currently beginning another round of organized soccer. This time, however, we chose a league that practices only twice a week and has no out-of-town games. This should go far in keeping mom sane, though there are bound to be some busy afternoons.

Making Activities Work

Over the years, besides soccer, our kids have done martial arts, baseball, dance, choir, drama, gymnastics, and piano. Many of these activities have been excellent experiences for our kids, and I'm glad that they've had them. But it takes thought and careful prioritizing to make it a positive experience for everyone. And remember—mom is part of everyone. If mom is being run ragged by kids' schedules, then something needs to change.

Starting Activities: One very simple way to make sports more doable for large families is to consider waiting until at least first grade to

If mom is being run ragged by kids' schedules, then something needs to change.

begin. We've done our share of preschool activities in the past, and I can totally understand the impulse to give little ones a head start, especially when they show a true interest in an activity. But over the years, I've become convinced that preschoolers could learn just as much about both sports and friendship by running around in the backyard playing with family and friends.

When we put our four-year-old in soccer, he had a great time running up and down the field, randomly kicking the ball towards whichever goal was most convenient. I paid $80 for that privilege and also got to hustle him to two practices and one game a week. It wasn't until he was at least seven that the rules of soccer actually meant anything to him. If I had it to do again, I would have just let him practice his soccer skills in the backyard with parents and older siblings until he was old enough to appreciate it.

We had a similar experience with piano lessons. One of our children learned to read at the age of four and is very musically inclined. We assumed that he would pick up on piano easily. But it took him twice as long as his older siblings to learn the notes, and he did not really start reading piano music until he was seven. On the other hand, our most gifted pianist (so far) didn't start lessons till age ten. At that age, she had the maturity and self-motivation to make tremendous strides in a short time.

Swimming was another thing we tried to do in an organized fashion at an early age. I learned the expensive way that the main goal of both Mommy and Me and preschool swimming lessons is simply to get children comfortable with water. Guess what? I can do that for free by simply getting into the pool and playing with my little ones.

No expensive classes. No hurrying to get to class on time. And it is a wonderful bonding activity—yes, even if I am tugging at my swimsuit and wishing a little less of my winter-white body was exposed to the world.

I'm not saying that preschool classes are always a waste. If you have the free time and the interest, give them a try. But most moms who are juggling more than a couple of kids would be happier having fewer must-show events during the week. And most preschoolers would be just as happy with a bit of extra time with mom or a casual play date with friends.

Choosing Activities: Once your kids are old enough to begin some extracurricular activities, think quality over quantity. Focus on activities that provide your child with the most enjoyment and the most value. Certainly kids need to try things to discover what they really love. And there will be a certain amount of error along with all that trial. (Hint: if your kid spends his ball games in the outfield trying to coax ants into his cap, baseball probably isn't his thing.)

Think of creative ways your child can try an activity without a lot of initial cost. One year, when we wanted our kids to be able to play baseball without the stress and cost and killer schedule of a team, we got together with a couple other families and played family baseball once a week. In that relaxed atmosphere, we had plenty of chances to help kids with their skills in a low-pressure sort of way. And it didn't cost us a dime. When we decided to sign up kids for "real" baseball, we knew who was interested and who wasn't.

Setting Limits: Here's a hard truth about having a large family: for everyone's sanity, you may need to limit the number of activities that children are allowed. Sure, you can push yourself to death to give your kids the "ideal" childhood. But guess what? The ideal childhood also allows time to climb trees and ride bikes and read comic books.

Overscheduled kids miss out on the chance to play dress up with their sisters and rassle with their brothers. Do you want your home to be an Indy-style refueling pit or a place to gather and relax?

To avoid overscheduling ourselves, my husband and I allow our kids one individual activity per year. Group activities such as weekly church youth group, monthly home school skate, Friday night soccer, and our weekly family swim time don't count. The one-activity limit is just for individual sports.

Because of this rule, kids are thoughtful about what they want to do. Sometimes they will make a choice they are unhappy with and will wistfully watch other kids play a sport they've belatedly decided they'd rather do. But that is part of life. There will be another chance in a few months to make another choice.

Staggering Activities: Another thing that helps our family juggle multiple schedules is to encourage children to pick sports and activities that start and end at different times in the year. Summer is the time for family camping and play in the backyard with brothers and sisters. We avoid organized sports during the summer. We let our kids sign up for spring soccer but not fall league. We save our fall and winter free time for activities at our local recreation center, such as swimming lessons, martial arts, and gymnastics.

When we were doing baseball, we had our younger children participate in a league that began a month later than the more serious league for older boys. This minimized the time we had multiple children going different places at the same time.

Choosing Short-Term Activities: Another great way to expose kids to different activities is to pick things that run for a brief period of time. Our recreation center has something called short sports. These sessions run once a week for just three weeks and allow kids to try five or six different activities in a fun, low-key way during each session.

Another brief activity that our children have been involved in over the years is Missoula Children's Theater. This is an intensive one-week theater experience. On Monday, kids audition for a theatrical production that will then be practiced every night all week, with performances scheduled for Saturday. To learn about Missoula events in your area, visit http://www.mctinc.org. Missoula week is very busy at our house, especially when multiple children are fortunate enough to get parts. But the brevity of the craziness makes it doable for me.

Another theater company in our town does similar productions, but they practice five nights a week for months before every play. As much as our children enjoy theater, this type of busyness would be way too much for our family. I'm glad that Missoula offers such a quality experience with such a brief investment of time.

> One very simple way to make sports more doable for large families is to consider waiting until at least first grade to begin.

Putting It All Together—What It Looks Like for Us

At the writing of this chapter, our eldest daughter is in college. We also have kids ages seventeen, sixteen, thirteen, twelve, ten, nine, nine, five, and three. Just before Christmas the twelve-, ten-, and nine-year-olds took swimming lessons at our local indoor pool. I signed up two kids each in two different levels of lessons in back-to-back half-hour time slots. That meant that all four kids completed their lessons in one hour's time twice a week. Basically, I was getting four kids' worth of activities for the same effort that it would have taken me to ferry kids one at a time. During that time, our other kids were free to run the track or swim, which they all enjoy.

I held off on starting the five-year-old in swimming lessons before Christmas, because her class was not available at that time and I didn't want to be stuck at the pool for hours on end. Once we got through Christmas craziness, I was able to find a swim lesson for her that ran at the same time and place as a martial arts class for my ten-year-old. Again, this gave a couple of kids the chance for an activity with no extra driving or time investment. Side note: my husband and I don't count swimming lessons as kids' individual activities, since they are something we require them to do for safety.

Our seventeen-year-old just completed a lifeguard class. She paid for most of it herself and drove herself, which made the twice-a-week, three-hour classes doable. We are pleased that she is interested in learning this skill that will help her earn college money.

We're about to begin soccer for three of the middle kids. That is a major time investment. But we're pleased with the low-key schedule this league has. As an added bonus, two of our boys are exactly the same age. We've requested that they be put on the same team so we'll only be committed to two teams, not three.

Once your kids are old enough to begin some extracurricular activities, think quality over quantity. Focus on activities that provide your child with the most enjoyment and the most value.

A fourth child expressed interest in soccer, mostly because all the siblings close to her age were doing it. But I knew from our Friday soccer games that she loses interest in the game after half an hour and heads for the playground. This year she already had taken two months of martial arts. So when she asked about soccer, I gently reminded her of this year's choice and assured her that she can do soccer next year if she'd like. She wasn't thrilled with my answer and, frankly, neither was I. I'd love to tell my kids yes all the time. But I knew I'd regret it if I didn't stick to our one-activity rule. If kids take the rule seriously, they're much less likely to constantly attempt to renegotiate. And adding a third soccer team to the soccer equation this year would have run me into the ground. That would have been a poor bargain for the family as a whole.

Expectations

When you're making decisions about activities for your children, ask yourself what kind of expectations you are teaching. If you always say yes no matter what the cost, are you really preparing your child for adulthood? Sure, we want our kids to have a can-do attitude. But some sports may help our kids develop very expensive tastes indeed.

This winter our sixteen-year-old son has been fortunate enough to take snowboarding lessons. This is not an activity we would usually be able to provide for our kids. Snowboarding is expensive and takes a great deal of time. He was fortunate enough to be offered a weekly ride by a friend's parents and had enough in savings to pay for the lessons himself. He's getting in on a really affordable homeschool special: lessons, equipment, and a lift pass for $25 a day.

Maybe he will be able to afford snowboarding as an adult. Maybe not. Once he has a family, his money may need to go for more mundane things like groceries and rent. We're thankful he's getting the opportunity, but we've encouraged him to enjoy it as a special gift without having the expectation that this will always be a part of his life.

Too many adults assume that expensive hobbies are their right in life, no matter how much debt they incur. I want our kids to see expensive hobbies and activities as bonus material—frills that are not absolutely essential to happiness. That way they will find happiness easier even if they do have budget limitations as adults.

Finding Money

It pays to think creatively when it comes to funding children's activities. Several of our children took a dance class for a couple of years, and I was able to get a tuition break by helping the director with costumes. For awhile the kids sang in a choir that charged half the tuition for second or subsequent children enrolled in the choir. I was able to do some computer work for the directors to cut the cost even more. To get deals like this, your best bet is to approach teachers who run their own classes and set their own fees. Your local YMCA might not be able to cut you a special deal.

For awhile we had four kids in piano. This was expensive, and I struggled to get kids to have their lessons complete by the time the teacher came each week. Finally, I decided to ask the teacher to come every two weeks. This cut the lesson cost by 50 percent and also gave the kids more time to learn each piece. This may not be an option to some teachers, but it made piano lessons much more possible for us. Another really great thing about our piano teacher is that she comes to our home, which means that I can carry on with my normal day while kids take their lessons.

Recently I hit upon another way to make our extracurricular activities more affordable. Before Christmas, when my mom asked for gift ideas for grandchildren, I suggested gift certificates to our local recreation center. These certificates were good for a variety of lessons including swimming, dance, gymnastics, martial arts, and even rock climbing. My mom loved having this chance to enrich her grandchildren's lives, and the kids had a great time taking classes that might not have otherwise fit into our budget.

Creative thinking can also save you money when it comes to equipment. If your child is interested in a musical instrument, consider borrowing or renting the instrument for a year or so before you buy. Lots of kids have initial interest in an activity and then burn out after a few months, leaving the parents in possession of all sorts of expensive equipment. Craigslist and eBay are great places to buy lightly used and

To avoid overscheduling ourselves, my husband and I allow our kids one individual activity per year. Because of this rule, kids are thoughtful about what they want to do.

abandoned equipment. Friends have also gifted us with hand-me-down rollerblades.

I've had great success buying soccer cleats on eBay. My favorite win was three pairs of cleats that turned out to be in my own hometown. The seller happily delivered them to my husband's business, which meant I didn't even have to pay shipping.

You may be able to ask your local pool what they do with long-abandoned swimwear. Sometimes it is given away or sold for very little money. One question (and a good hot-water washing of course!) can get you some really nice things.

I've also found karate outfits, swimsuits, and bike helmets by looking online or at local yard sales or thrift stores. Recently, I scored three nice modest swimsuits at a thrift store for a grand total of $15. Sometimes you'll need to buy things new. But it is usually worth it to check out secondhand options first.

Logistics

Once you've decided which activities fit your family best, think next about the children who will need to tag along to the various activities. During sports season, I keep the back of my van fully stocked with everything my family will need while waiting out a practice or a game in the cold or heat. In a plastic bin, I stash granola bars, fruit snacks, water bottles, Legos, art supplies, and extra pants and/or diapers for toddlers. In the back, I stash chairs, old quilts, and extra coats.

*Recently, I hit upon another way to make
our extracurricular activities more affordable.
Before Christmas, when my mom asked for gift
ideas for grandchildren, I suggested gift
certificates to our local recreation center.*

I even have a secret weapon with which to combat porta-potty nastiness. There's nothing worse than a stinky porta-potty that has been recklessly used by a bunch of ten-year-old boys. Sometimes public restrooms can be ridiculously far from ball fields. Last year one practice field was utterly barren. No bathrooms. No bushes. Nothing. Literally the only option at this field was to pack all the young ones into the van in the middle of the game, drive a quarter mile to the nearest gas station, and take care of business there. More than once it caused me to miss my son's at-bat, which was more than a little frustrating.

That was when I conceived my handy-dandy potty kit. We are fortunate enough to have a van that has a big empty space behind the back seat, along with nice dark-tinted windows. In the back of the van I keep a potty kit. It consists of the basin from under a child's potty chair, some plastic sacks, a couple of cut-in-half diapers, and some disinfecting wipes.

Here's my trick: I put half a diaper in the potty seat before the child uses it. The diaper soaks up the moisture—no sloshy liquid to spill, nothing to dump. Just sack up the diaper, wipe down the basin with a disinfecting wipe, and sack up the wipe. Then bag the basin for the next emergency.

The child has perfect privacy and much cleaner surroundings than the porta-potty. And I don't spend two innings of a baseball game trekking a little kid to and from the potty. By the time kids are old enough to object to this system, they're also old enough to hold it for awhile. It works out perfectly. I take the kids to the bathroom if it isn't a mile away (carrying hand sanitizer in my pocket!). But at least a couple of times a season my potty kit is a real sanity-saver.

Another challenge of having a bunch of kids in the same sport all at once is trying to remember which day you are supposed to bring snacks. My friend Carmen often has five kids in soccer at a time. She routinely signs up to provide the snacks for all her kids' teams on opening day of soccer season. Providing six-dozen snacks all in one day is a formidable task, but she finds it easier than trying to remember all season which day is her snack day for five different teams.

Are Extracurricular Activities Really Essential?

Even when done thoughtfully, extracurricular activities can still sometimes make you crazy, especially if you're a homebody like me. Jeana, a mother of four, recently had to eliminate all organized sports from her family's life for financial reasons, and she has been amazed at the blessing in disguise that it has been:

> I recall reading an article last year about a family whose children had no outside activities other than music lessons. At the time I thought that seemed so extreme—children need other activities! [But] that is exactly what we do now and it's perfect for us. I admit, though, that I never would have given those other things up had God not wrung them from my clenched fists.
>
> I remember too many times that I snapped at and scolded my children in an effort to get them out the door once again; and how many times I ran into a friend or neighbor and thought how I would like to spend time with them or help

them in some way or just build a friendship, but my schedule
wouldn't allow it. I remember feeling something wasn't right,
when I was committing to outside ministries or services but I
never seemed to have time for the people God had placed right
in front of me.

In the last year our kids have gotten fewer treats, outings,
time with friends, activities—all of those things you think kids
"need"—and they've never been happier. You really do find more
pleasure in the little things when you remove the big stuff.

Cutting out all activities is not a choice everyone would make. But
it is a viable one for many people and one that gives you back two
precious commodities: time and money. While writing this chapter and
sharing some of our past experience with activities, I've been struck
with how many things our kids have been able to do over the years.
And by being creative and keeping our family's goals clearly in mind, we
were able to do it without sacrificing our budget or our sanity.

AFFORDABLE VACATIONS

Is a Disney Vacation a Childhood Essential?

Awhile back, I asked a young man to tell me about his favorite childhood memories. I was especially interested in his viewpoint because he had been adopted at the age of twelve. He was obviously a high-functioning person, and I wondered what his family had done to help him feel so connected to them, even though his childhood with them had been much shorter than the average kid's. The man smiled and said without hesitation that his best memories were of camping trips with his family.

Now before you shout "better dead than camping," let me assure you that not all family vacations have to involve Coleman stoves and walls that you'd better not touch if you want your sleeping bag to stay dry in the night. But I am convinced that vacation memories are especially wonderful things for children to carry with them into adulthood.

Vacation is a time when the regular tasks and responsibilities are suspended for awhile, when time can be spent on pure fun. Studies have shown that the memories people are most likely to remember from childhood are the unexpected things—the times that surprise us or provide an interesting break in the routine. I know that vacation time provided some of my richest childhood memories. How about you?

If you're not a camper, don't despair. Great kid-friendly vacations can be had only steps from a bathroom, TV, or microwave. But I'd encourage you to keep an open mind. Something you've never considered may just be a perfect vacation for your whole family, including mom.

Family-Friendly Destinations

Many people think of Disneyworld as *the* family vacation destination. People save up their money and plot their course and pour out buckets of money in four brief days. I know . . . people rave about how much fun it is. But I can't help wondering if they rave partly just to justify the cost.

When I was a kid, we went on vacations every year. Usually, we drove from Missouri to Idaho to visit my mom's family. Once we went camping in the Ozark Mountains. Another time we went to California to Disneyland. Here's what I remember about my famed Disneyland experience: I was nine at the time, Space Mountain was fun, and the Swiss Family Robinson tree house was beyond awesome. But my mom did a lot of waiting around with the teeny kids while the bigger ones rode on rides. It was hot as blazes, I was forever thirsty, and it seemed to me that most of our time was spent waiting in line.

I can understand the reasoning that led my parents to give us that childhood experience. Disney is such a hyped part of childhood that people fear they're gypping their kids if they don't give them that experience. But that time was exceedingly brief, and I am certain my childhood would have been just as good without that very expensive forty-eight hours of my life.

Now let me tell you some of my very best vacation memories. I remember camping in a borrowed army surplus tent with my family, someplace in the middle of Kansas, and singing hymns in the dark at bedtime. Every time I sing "The Old Rugged Cross," I am taken back to that time and remember the sweet sound of my parents' voices mingling with all the little ones. I remember swimming with my brothers and sisters in a KOA campground swimming pool. I remember fishing with my dad and hooking a dead fish that floated past our boat.

I remember playing school in an old abandoned farm building with my Idaho cousins. I remember sleeping bags all over my grandmother's attic floor and giggling with cousins until our folks called up the stairs for quiet. I remember that my Idaho grandmother always got kittens just for me when we came to visit every summer. Once I dressed the poor kittens in doll clothes, fed them marshmallows, and then wheeled them around in a baby carriage until one threw up.

As memories go, these may seem pretty random. But they share a common theme—family, not Disney princesses.

> Disney is such a hyped part of childhood
> that people fear they're gypping their kids if
> they don't give them that experience.

Disney is a perfectly reasonable option if you can afford it. But there are many other great options out there that will be just as meaningful to your children. The ideal large-family vacation will, of course, fit into your budget. It will include activities that are interesting to a broad range of kids. There will also be times that are rejuvenating to mom. Let's face it, vacationing with a growing family can mean big work. But with some careful planning, there can be times in each day that are enjoyable for parents as well.

Ideally, there will also be times each day for the whole family to be together. Too often at amusement parks, parents have to divide and conquer, one parent with the big kids and the other with the ones who are too young to ride the rides. Think about activities that the whole family loves.

One of our favorite ways to spend our time while on vacation is to hang out on the beach. Home base is a couple of camp chairs for the readers in the family. People fan out all over the beach to build sand castles, ride bikes, hunt shells, and take pictures. We may be spread all over the beach, but there is still a sense of family. We can look up and see each other, and easily check back in to chat and get snacks as needed.

Getting There

A huge consideration when planning a family vacation is location. How close is your destination? How will you get there? Airfare for eight to Disney World might be beyond most people's annual trip budgets. But that doesn't mean you can't go anywhere. Many families plan great vacations that are within one- or two-days' drive of their own homes.

When I was a child, my parents' annual trek from Missouri to Idaho took about thirty hours. They often took turns driving day and night. Traveling that far with a bunch of kids could not have been easy. But my mom always packed goodies to make the long hours in the car more bearable. And the fun we had once we reached Granny's house always had us looking forward to our next trip.

Whether flying or driving, it pays to plan. Before each driving trip, I visit the dollar store and come up with goodies and small toys to hand out every couple of hours on the way there. Good options include markers and paper, non-messy non-salty snacks, and small handheld games. Our kids have enjoyed a small round gadget called 20 Questions. The whole family can listen in as this game is played. We've also enjoyed books on tape and DVDs played on my laptop on a stand at the front of the van. We save movies for trips farther than two hours away, and we alternate movies with other activities. But DVD players definitely make long drives easier for little kids.

When traveling with little ones, it is important to stay flexible. You may need to stop more often than you'd originally imagined. One parent may need to sit in back with the baby to stave off meltdowns. Driving during the night or during your baby's nap time is also a good strategy.

Last year, I flew to Ethiopia with our two- and five-year-olds, which

*Whether flying or driving, it pays to plan.
Before each driving trip, I visit the dollar store
and come up with goodies and small toys to hand
out every couple of hours on the way there.*

is a flight of nearly thirty hours. We packed fanny packs for our little girls. They contained tiny toys, snacks, paper, markers, tape, and lip balm. The tape and the lip balm were the biggest hits. When the novelty of their goodies wore out, I pulled other toys out of my own backpack. The girls had a few unhappy moments, and I was thankful for every minute they spent napping, but they did really well overall. Thanks to my secret chocolate stash—an essential for any mom traveling with little ones—I did pretty well too.

Lodging Options

Getting to your destination is only part of the battle. Deciding where to stay can take some major planning. Here, I'll describe some of the most common options and the pros and cons that they have for large families.

Campgrounds

Pros: Campgrounds are one of the most affordable options for families. Campsites with electricity and water can be had for less than $30 a night. There are usually playgrounds for children as well as plenty of opportunity for outdoor play. Kids tend to love camping, especially when it comes to marshmallows and hot dogs around the campfire. Pets are welcome at campgrounds.

Some campgrounds (including the Oregon Park system) offer the option of yurt camping. Yurts are a cross between a tent and a cabin, with locking doors and beds that are already set up. Many yurts sleep five to eight people. All you'll need to bring is bedding and food. If you've never camped before, yurt camping may be a nice easy way to see what it is like without actually having to buy a lot of equipment.

Cons: Camping is a ton of work for parents, especially if you are tent camping. It also involves buying or borrowing a fair bit of equipment. You'll have less protection from the weather. Tent camping in the rain is no vacation, no matter how determined you are to be cheerful. You also have your entire family in very close proximity. You may decide that it is worth it for short periods of time, just to give your children the experience. When we were tent camping, we made it a tradition to stay in a hotel with a pool on the final night of a camping trip, just as a nice recharge for the parents. Other sanity savers include packing lots of easy-cook canned food and going out to eat once a day while camping.

If your budget is tight, you just can't beat camping. Early in our marriage, John and I camped in a little four-man tent. Once the kids started coming, we bought a bigger tent, which worked well for awhile. About the time we found ourselves camping with giant mosquitoes in rain that would not stop, with three little kids, one of whom was crawling everywhere, I realized that I was getting burned out on tent camping, restaurants or not.

We upgraded to an old sixteen-foot Kit travel trailer. There was no bathroom, but the kitchen was adorable and blessedly dry, even in a rainstorm. One of my favorite camping memories is of an afternoon spent in the dry trailer in the driving rain, reading books and contentedly looking out the rain-misted windows. At $500, that trailer was a real bargain and gave us several more years of happy camping.

As I have gotten older and our family has gotten bigger, I've found myself getting more and more picky about my camping experience. We currently own a twenty-eight-foot travel trailer that sleeps ten, complete with a microwave, a fridge, and a full bathroom. Our two teenaged boys pitch a tent nearby, enabling them to stay up till all hours, playing games without disturbing younger siblings. We also have a screen tent that is perfect for games in the evenings. The little kids can go to sleep in the trailer while much fun is still being had by the bigger people outside.

The thing you have to prepare for when camping is that the best of times happen shoulder to shoulder with the frustrating ones, and it is anyone's guess which you'll encounter in the next second. A minute from now, will you be blissfully paging through *O, The Oprah Magazine*, while kids happily build sand castles at your feet? Or will you be looking balefully at the tiny spot in the far distance that is the outhouse as the three-year-old cries and does a desperate potty dance at your feet?

Will you snap the perfect shot of the baby eating her first s'more? Or will she drop her treat on the ground just as you lift the camera, then throw a thrashing mega-tantrum when you toss the pine-needle-encrusted mess to the dog?

Many of our family vacation memories involve camping, and I am glad for the kids' sake that we have been able to camp with them. But as I get older and our family gets larger, I find myself longing more and more for vacations that actually feel like a vacation to me, thus my love affair with our vacation rental house.

Rental Houses
Pros: A few years ago, on a whim, I investigated rental-house options near our favorite coastal vacation spot. I was amazed to find that if we rented a house off-season (between October and April), we could rent an entire four-bedroom house overlooking the ocean for $150 a night. In contrast, two hotel rooms that we rented recently cost $190 a night and didn't give us a quarter of the space.

A carefully chosen rental house can be a wonderful option for a large family. Bedding is usually provided. The full kitchen means you don't have to eat out every meal. Many rentals contain nice amenities such as Jacuzzis, DVD players, and TVs. Little ones will have quiet places to nap while older ones are safely contained. And your family will have plenty of room to spread out.

Cons: We have enjoyed our vacation rental so much that it is now an annual tradition. However it does have some downsides. Many rentals do not allow you to bring pets. The cost is quite a bit more expensive than camping. You'll need to watch your children carefully to make sure things are not broken in play. Many times, cleanup at the end of a stay can be labor intensive. Our rental charges us $150 if we do not clean up after ourselves. Since checkout time is 11 a.m., we have to get up pretty darned early to get all that linen washed before we leave. Every year, I think we should just pay the $150 and leave the laundry. But then my frugal side kicks in, and we scurry around that last morning, doing it ourselves anyway.

We've also made a habit of bringing along half a dozen sleeping bags. That way, we can wash half the bedding the day before we leave and have some of the kids sleep on the floor in sleeping bags that last night to keep the bedding clean.

Hotels
Pros: Hotels allow you to travel without having to gather lots of gear. Choosing a hotel that offers a free breakfast will cut down on the cost of the trip. Hotel pools are wonderful places for rowdy kids to burn off energy while mom sits and reads a book. Since most hotel rooms do not have kitchenettes, you have a great excuse to eat every meal out—a plus in the minds of many frazzled moms.

Cons: The biggest downside of a hotel is the expense. If you tell most hotels that you have more than four kids, you'll probably be required to rent two hotel rooms. Hotels can feel confining to energetic children. After a day of driving, they'll be bouncing around the room, which can

> I was amazed to find that if we rented a [beach]
> house off-season . . . we could rent an entire
> four-bedroom house overlooking the ocean for
> $150 a night. A carefully chosen rental house can
> be a wonderful option for a large family.

be disruptive to the people in the next room, or at least aggravating to parents who are trying to keep a lid on the chaos.

The noise can be even more frustrating when you're trying to get a baby or toddler to go to sleep with other siblings still awake in the room. We almost always bring a small fan with us on trips, no matter where we're staying. The white noise of the fan at bedtime muffles the sound of other family members who are still awake, as well as being a more familiar background than the creaks and squeaks of a strange location.

Sometimes your only lodging option on a trip is a hotel. A few years ago, we found a great hotel in Jackson, Wyoming, with a room that had two queen beds, a hide-a-bed, and a porta-crib. By planning our trip three days before the official start of the summer season, we got the off-season rate of $89 a night. Not bad for a room big enough to fit seven people.

Some hotels have suites that are suitable for a large family. Other hotels may allow you to sleep an extra child or two in a room for an extra fee. But, in most cases, large families are forced to rent two rooms, which can get pricey as well as being inconvenient if the two rooms you've been assigned end up being ten rooms apart. If you have teenagers like we do, it may not be a big deal to have them on the other end of the building. If all your children are young, dad and mom will need to split up at bedtime, which is not exactly ideal. Be sure to specify when making reservations that you will need adjoining rooms. You'll be more likely to actually get this if you make your reservations over the phone instead of online.

Lodging Option: Rooming with Family

Pros: Depending on your destination, you might have the option of staying with family or friends on vacation. This option has many advantages if you have the right kind of family—and if you can be a good guest! The price is right. You'll be able to cook in your family's kitchen. If there is a backyard, your children will be able to play outdoors. And staying with family will maximize your visiting time.

Depending on your destination, you might have the option of staying with family or friends on vacation. It can get stressful to keep a bunch of active children from knocking over Grandma's Precious Moments collection or from petting Fifi to death.

Cons: If your family is very large, your relatives might find it overwhelming to have you visit for more than a day or two. After all, you've gotten used to the noise level of your brood. Grandma and Grandpa love your children, but they are most likely used to a much quieter existence. Physical space in the home may also be lacking. It can get stressful to keep a bunch of active children from knocking over Grandma's Precious Moments collection or from petting Fifi to death.

There are things you can do, however, to extend your welcome at a friend's or relative's home. Above all, be flexible and respectful of your host's preferences. It may be wise to plan activities here and there than don't involve your hosts, just to give them a little break. Also be sure to invite your hosts out to dinner a time or two. Supply some of the groceries. Consider stopping for pizza on the way home from an outing so that your hosts will have one less meal to prepare. And by all means, encourage your kids to pitch in and express their thanks for the hospitality as well. If you have the right kind of family and treat them with respect, you'll probably be invited back again and again.

What to Do When You Get There

Another consideration for family vacations is what to do once you arrive at your destination. Even affordable activities can add up fast. I can't tell you how many times someone has mentioned an activity that is only $5 a person. But I have ten kids, which makes $5 a person look like much less of a bargain. I will only spend that much on a truly worthwhile activity.

Here's where family passes really shine. We love visiting the Oregon Coast Aquarium. Instead of buying day passes for each person totaling well over $100, we simply buy a one-year family membership for $90. Usually we end up going two or three times during the week we're visiting the ocean. If we make our next trip within a year, we can even get several more visits in for that same $90.

Zoos and children's museums are other places that offer similar bargains for families. Usually the family membership costs the same whether you're a family of three or a family of twelve. When you count the cost of day passes for a crowd, that will usually translate to money savings for a large family. Some zoos and museums even have reciprocal or partner memberships with other zoos and museums across the country. If you're traveling, it pays to see if there are other places you might be able to visit using memberships you already have.

My friend Jeana talks about getting the most out of field trips and excursions with her family:

> *Whether it's a field trip or a vacation, with kids or without, we go around and have everyone say the one thing they want to*

do most. Then we try to make sure we at least do those things (taking into account, of course, cost, location, etc.). Mom and Dad have the right of veto, but we try to hit at least the top picks of each person. Otherwise, the more assertive people get to do everything they want and the shy ones get overlooked. Or we hit one section of the zoo, meander through, then, when we're all heading for the car at the end of the day, exhausted, someone bursts into tears and wails, "But I wanted to see the PYTHON!" This could still happen, but if you used this method, at least you don't feel as coldhearted when you turn them down; you simply point out that the one thing they picked was the kangaroo.

Whether it's a field trip or a vacation, with kids or without, we go around and have everyone say the one thing they want to do most.

Kate, a mother of four, describes a creative way that her folks made the most of museum trips with a big crowd:

When we were little, my folks did not have much money, but they did have a desire to raise "cultured" children. We traveled as much as possible on a shoestring budget and toured every single museum in every town and city we visited. We couldn't afford pricey souvenirs, so my mother made it fun in other ways. Every time we went to a museum, we visited the gift shop first! We spent a few dollars buying postcards of paintings and artifacts from the museum—maybe three postcards for each kid. Then we went on a hunt in the museum to see who could find the objects in her postcards first! At night, we would glue the cards into a journal and write about the particular place we had visited. These days, with four kids, we don't do much traveling, and I have to admit that their many sporting events make it hard to prioritize "culture" in this way. Still, we go to museums whenever we get the chance, and my kids love to play this game themselves, even the moody teenagers.

Planning a vacation for a growing family takes a little more doing, but it is so worth the effort. Vacations supply our children—and us—with rich and wonderful memories that will remain forever, even when the s'mores fall into the fire.

THE SUPERMOM MYTH

Where Is My Supersuit?

Myths swirl thick around mega-moms. I can barely get through the grocery store without someone commenting on my candidacy for either the loony bin or sainthood. I'm not sure which perception I dislike more. People have a hard time seeing mothers of large families as normal. It's a shame, because not only does it intimidate other women into thinking that they don't have what it takes to mother another child or two but it also separates mothers of large families from the support they might gain from other mothers.

Jenni Wilson, a mother who is expecting her twelfth child, says she feels less free to share her normal struggles as a mother:

> *Do I say nothing and let them keep me on the pedestal, never able to share real prayer requests or achieve any kind of intimacy? Or should I be truthful and make them question my sanity? Just how transparent can I be? Will my desire for friendship cause me to be so blatantly blunt that they instead think "Wow . . . she never should have had all those kids! Maybe I should find that Department of Social Services number . . ."*

It bothers Jenni when people think that she had a large family because she was born with unusual patience or organization or spirituality.

> *If I do, in fact, display any of those characteristics, it is through the constant stretching and pummeling that my flesh has gone through in the process. And this is the crux of my reality . . . the one thing I want folks to know: I am the same as you. We all have opportunities for growth. I call mine children.*

Dispelling Myths: Are You Nuts?

The insanity question is one of the more insulting questions that moms of many face. Yes, the question is usually tossed out with a laugh. But many people quite honestly see only a few explanations for having a big crew: faulty birth control, extreme stupidity, or outright insanity.

To be sure, lots of women have a surprise pregnancy or two. Our second child was only eleven months old when we discovered we were expecting number three. But there are plenty of women out there who are intentional in growing a larger family. People today have a hard time wrapping their minds around that.

America is a self-indulgent society. The more children you have, the more demands there are on your time and the less time you have for yourself. Sure, you can still arrange time now and then to recharge—I'll talk about ways to stay sane in future chapters. But parenting a large family chips away at your free time. That scares people, plain and simple.

Mothers of many will quickly admit that parenting more children is more work. But they will also tell you that the variety that comes with a big crew is a wonderful thing. When one kid is going through a difficult phase, there's always another child who is easier to parent at the moment and who can help you recharge a bit. Jeanne, a mother of six, also relishes the variety in her life:

I think it keeps me on my toes having to fill so many different roles for their different ages; for example, teaching one to ride a bike and another to drive a car. Another benefit is that I am always "the best Mom in the world" to at least one kid, and often as many as three or four of them might think of me with high regard. What touches my heart more than anything is to see the relationships that blossom between the children and to catch those moments when they let genuine love and caring slip through. I hope that those moments will keep them close to each other, no matter what corner of this world they land in.

What Does It Take to Raise a Growing Family?

Parents of larger families are a diverse bunch. Some of us homeschool. Some don't. Many of us are religious, though not all. Some have a deep well of patience. Some—like me—wish for more every day. But we all share a genuine delight in children.

Does that mean we love playing endless games of Candyland? Does that mean we can wake up twelve times in the night with the baby and still be smiling? No way. But it does mean that our children's funny sayings make us laugh, their little bodies make us want to hug, and their accomplishments, big or small, make us want to cheer.

Inventiveness: One of the things that amazes me about kids is their uniqueness. Even my kids who are biologically related to each other can be so different in their needs and motivations. People imagine that by the time parents have three or four kids, they have parenting figured out. To a certain degree, this is true. But the very individuality of children will always keep parents scrambling. Count on it.

There is no one-size-fits-all parenting. A parenting trick that works for an older sibling might not be effective with a younger one.

You'll always be more effective when you
aim for your child's funny bone.

Inventiveness is an important skill for a mother to develop. Notice I say "develop." You don't have to be born with endless creativity. It is enough to be willing to learn along the way.

Flexibility: You'll probably have an easier time parenting a bunch of kids if you learn to major in the majors. My own mom often puts things into perspective by saying, "It doesn't affect your salvation."

It helps to be able to let little things slide. At our house, we joke that a meal isn't complete until someone has spilled their drink. The little kids are glad when every now and then it is a big person making a mess. No one likes to feel like a klutz, not even a four-year-old. But if we can laugh at ourselves instead of stomping and grumping when the inevitable spills happen, we have demonstrated an important skill to our kids.

Humor: The other day my nine-year-old was having one of those terrible horrible no-good days. He was picking fights with everyone in sight and complaining about everything. I grabbed him and playfully wrestled him over to the couch for a snuggle. He put up a token resistance, just to prove his bad humor was serious. But by the time I had him on the couch, he was trying to hide a grin, and we were well on the way to a better mood.

First I let him spout off what he was mad about: a brother not sharing a video game. I asked him for a solution. He suggested that the unkind brother make his bed. I countered that the unkind brother really should shovel out the horse pen.

"Yeah!" he said enthusiastically.

"Or what about the driveway?" I said. "I really think it needs to be scrubbed. Maybe with a toothbrush."

His lips twitched, but he again agreed enthusiastically. We went on in that vein for a couple of minutes, suggesting increasingly silly punishments for the selfish brother, with each new over-the-top consequence bringing on more giggles.

Soon his mood was receptive enough that I was able to remind him that people do not always have to share their treasured possessions and that he himself sometimes did not share. We brainstormed things he might be able to offer the brother in trade for sharing the game for awhile. Within minutes, his mood had turned around enough that he was able to go and try again with his brother, using the ideas we'd discussed. I would never have influenced his mood that powerfully with a stern "buck up—your brother doesn't have to share" lecture.

I am a fairly serious person and, at times, have to remind myself to go for the laugh instead of a lecture. My husband gets corny with the kids effortlessly. When he does, the children glow, no matter how much I'm rolling my eyes in the background at his silliness. Humor is one of a parent's most powerful allies. You'll always be more effective when you aim for your child's funny bone.

Smiling Eyes: Sometimes a day can get so busy, and we can get so preoccupied with all the things that we must get done that we can forget to smile into our children's eyes. We can forget to make that heart connection. Even on busy days, when my kids come to me to share a story or ask a question, I try to "twinkle" at them—to let them know that I am glad to be looking at them.

If a kid is cranky and resists "twinkling" back at me, I'll tickle him or spin him around or do something else that is silly or unexpected—anything to make him crack a smile. The minute or two it takes to make that connection is so worth it.

Dispelling Myths: "You Must Be So Organized!"

When women talk about having more children, most wonder about issues surrounding time and organization. Will I be so overwhelmed with laundry and cooking and working that the fun goes by the wayside? Will I have enough time to play with my children? Will I still be able to listen to them talk to me at bedtime? Will I have to live by a schedule just to survive?

People think that parents of many must just be born organized. No way. Though some people are natural organizers, most of us learn organizational skills from sheer necessity. In fact, I think that working mothers and mothers of large families are forced to learn a similar set of skills. Chances are, if you're currently juggling a career and a couple of kids, you already have many of the skills you'll need to raise another child or two.

Learning to Say No

At the heart of organizing your time is keeping your priorities clearly in mind. By the fourth or fifth child, most parents have come to grips with the fact that they can't do everything. Deciding what not to do allows you to make time for what is most important to you.

Only you can decide what is important to you and how much you can happily let go. If you're feeling stressed by the demands of your life, instead of vowing to get up earlier and work harder, take a careful look at the most stressful times of your day and pick a few tasks not to do.

An example from my life is the laundry. My mom taught me to sort laundry the traditional way: whites, lights, mediums, darks, and towels. As a new wife, I dutifully emulated my mom's approach. A few kids later, I got lax and tried the "grab any heap and chuck it in the washer" approach. To my surprise, the laundry didn't look much different.

Sure, there were those few rare occasions when I forgot about

*If you're feeling stressed by the demands of your
life, instead of vowing to get up earlier and work harder,
take a careful look at the most stressful times of your
day and pick a few tasks not to do.*

that new red shirt and my (very secure) hubby ended up wearing pink
underwear to work. But those times were rare. My casual approach
saved minutes every day and decreased our quality of life not one bit.

I also avoid the dry cleaners. I have literally been to the dry cleaners
twice in twenty years. Occasionally, I check laundry labels when I dry my
clothes, but mostly I buy what I want at the store and throw it all in the
wash. Either it lives or it dies. My teen daughters and I do avoid tossing
sweaters and snug shirts in the dryer, but the majority of our clothes
survive machine wash/tumble dry.

Another concept that decreases time in the laundry room is the
reusable towel. We hang towels on hooks in our bathrooms and use
them two or three times before we toss them in the wash. That tip alone
probably saves us three or four loads of laundry a week. Think about it:
most of the time when you're using a bath towel, you're wrapping it
around a fresh-washed body. What's to get dirty?

I also avoid ironing. I keep a mini ironing board tucked in a corner
for the occasional ironing project, but I use it maybe four times a year.
Most stuff that requires an iron looks just fine when tossed in the
dryer for fifteen minutes and then hung up. Even a crisply ironed shirt
develops wrinkles as soon as you buckle yourself into the car anyway.
It's fine with me if my blouses are smooth but not crisp. I do iron the
occasional badly lying collar. But most of the time, a tumble dry and a
prompt hang up avoids ironing entirely.

It goes without saying that knits are an essential part of my
wardrobe. If putting on a crisply ironed shirt is one of your great

pleasures, then ironing is not one of the things you'll want to cut out of your life. But being casual about laundry has not impacted my family's life in any measurable way except to give me time to do things I enjoy more.

Other examples of chores that can be reevaluated include bed making and dusting. We dust maybe once a month or so, and I make my bed every other day or so. But I don't require my kids to make their beds except when company comes over.

I like to vacuum my living room every day, but I'm somewhat casual about kitchen-floor sweeping. It happens every day or two, but with my huge crew, twice a day would barely be enough to keep it looking really nice. I have a friend who grew up in Korea, where everyone takes off shoes indoors and it is the housewife's duty to keep the floor spotless. Several times she has picked up a broom and swept my kitchen because it feels terrible on her feet. Obviously casual floor care would not work for her.

The trick is to thoughtfully select what you can let go to streamline your day. Remember, if you decide to let go of a task, don't hang onto any false guilt over it. You are making a conscious choice to free up your time—time to chat with a child or play a game or read a chapter of a book; time to walk down the lane and moo at the cows with your preschooler. It's all about priorities.

Dispelling Myths: "You Must Be So Patient!"

The other morning we began our normal day of school optimistically. I settled my two nine-year-old sons near me at the dining room table, since they do best when near me. They usually take two or three hours to complete their school for the day. One boy settled down to work, but the other one was just not in the game. He yawned. He twitched. He went to the bathroom. He stared off into space. He broke his pencil.

He sharpened it. Easy review problems made his eyes so wide that you'd have thought he was seeing martians.

It took him three full hours to complete two short pages of math—three full hours during which I reminded, cajoled, redirected, and explained. Three full hours during which I tried more or less successfully to smile pleasantly while repeating a trillion variations of "pay attention, honey." Three full hours during which I resisted the urge to beat my head on any hard surface in sight.

By the end of three hours, I was bubbling like a volcano ready to erupt. Patience was not even on my radar screen; I was frustrated with everything—with my child, with the other children who interrupted the endless math lesson, and, most of all, with myself, for being so darned frustrated.

I was not living up to my expectations for myself as a mother. After all, I've been a mom for nineteen years and a homeschooling mom for a dozen. I know by now that some days are better than others. Some days children just have a hard time focusing. Yet here I sat, like Mount Vesuvius ready to erupt. Shouldn't I have this patience thing figured out by now?

That's when reality clobbered me over the head. If I still struggle with patience after twenty years as a mom, I may never actually master patience. That was a tough fact to face.

Yet, when I replayed that morning in my head, I realized I was judging myself too harshly. After all, despite how I'd felt on the inside, I'd had some success on the outside. I'd maintained a relatively even tone of voice all morning long. I'd smiled. I'd hugged. I'd teased. I'd been firm when I needed to be and encouraging as often as possible. My kid hadn't seen Mount Vesuvius; he'd seen smiling eyes and steady guidance.

I'd love it if my insides matched my outsides all the time. I'd love it if I could actually feel serene all the time instead of just faking serenity. But despite what others assume about me, endless serenity is not my personal reality as a mother.

Maybe that's the heart of patience: refusing to be sucked down into negativity and instead choosing kindness; not avoiding the negative emotions—wouldn't that take a lobotomy?—but resisting them, rising above them, and prevailing over them.

I have a mental image of a patient mother. She never has to beat back frustration. In my image, that mother doesn't have to choose patience; she exudes it naturally from every tight, well-toned pore. Since I often have to fight for my patience, I've sometimes felt inadequate as a mother. But like the airbrushed thighs of models in *Glamour* magazine, I've come to realize that the smiling image of motherly serenity is unrealistic. Maybe even the most patient of mothers churns inside sometimes.

And maybe, just maybe, faking patience is good enough some days— to modulate the tone of my voice to approximate calm, to smile instead of letting the welling frustration spill out, and to tickle a kid instead of growling.

To be sure, there are times when a mother's indignation is righteous. I believe God gives moms instincts about the behavior of their children. Mothers should not have to tolerate sass. When our mouths hang open and our eyebrows go up because something nasty just came out of our child's mouth, then it's not about patience. At times like that it is our job to look our kids in the eye and say, "No way. As your mom, I deserve respect."

But plenty of the little irritations in life are related to broken dishes and lost shoes and forgotten multiplication tables—normal kid stuff. That's when it's time to take a deep breath and summon up that calm voice from somewhere inside so I can smile at that unhappy little one, and hunt down the shoes, or teach him how to sweep up the mess, or drill four-times-seven yet again.

Am I going to be able to do this all the time? No! I'm a human, not a saint. Sometimes Mount Vesuvius does erupt, whether the child deserves it or not. Then I take a deep breath, look my child in the eye, and apologize. I explain to my child that moms are human too, and resolve to try to do better next time.

I try every day to be more patient. But I also forgive myself for occasionally losing it. And when I manage to fake patience in a time of frustration, I'll count it a victory instead of beating myself up for not living up to my own image of perfect motherhood.

Jenni, my friend, says she struggles with her flaws as well:

> *As the mother of almost twelve, I can say with all certainty that the most amazing part of having a large family is the fact that it drives you to your knees before the Father so often. There is no self-delusion that you can somehow "be enough" for your children . . . that you can somehow meet their needs . . . because it's apparent 24/7 that you can't. Becoming a parent exposes flaws I might never see otherwise. Each child reflects just how well I am doing, and with so many, it's pretty much like living in a carnival house of mirrors. It can be cripplingly humbling sometimes, but it keeps me dependent upon His grace, and His grace alone.*

Finding Patience: Avoiding Volcano Moments

Which moments in life leave you most frustrated? Think over the last forty-eight hours. When did you find yourself slamming doors and muttering under your breath? Don't discount the possibility that some of your anger may have been richly deserved by your child. If your child is being disrespectful, don't tell yourself that you should be more patient. Deal with your child's misbehavior.

There are times, however, when at least some of the problem may lie with mom. For years, a major trouble point for me was getting everyone out of the house on time for activities: church, a baseball game, or a doctor's appointment. At times like that, the kids seemed to move like turtles that had stepped in cement. Inevitably someone would lose their shoes or need to go potty at the last minute or be hunting for a jacket three minutes after the last possible time we could get out the door and still be on time.

Just as predictably, I would lose my cool, berating the unhappy slowpokes all the way out the door and several miles down the road. Then guilt would set in and I'd end up apologizing. In my heart I knew that part of the problem rested with me.

I came up with several solutions. First, I began doing as much ahead of time as possible. I set out Sunday clothes on Saturday night, right down to tights, socks, and shoes. I began serving cold cereal on Sunday mornings to gain more time. No sense making Sunday harder by adding waffles and syrup to the mix.

To make sporting events easier, I washed uniforms the day before. I purchased team snacks several days before I needed them. I left the lawn chairs in the van all of soccer season instead of loading them into the van each time I needed them.

I also changed my aim. Instead of aiming to get out the door five minutes before I had to get out the door, I started aiming to leave half an hour sooner. Don't get me wrong: I've never managed to actually leave half an hour early. But often I manage to walk out the door five or ten minutes ahead of schedule. After years of unsuccessfully trying to beat the clock, let me tell you, that's a sweet, sweet feeling.

This Room Is a Wreck!: Another anger trigger of mine happened consistently at bedtime. I'd come into my children's rooms after lights out, mentally prepared for a few sweet moments kneeling next to their beds for a bedtime chat. Instead, I'd find myself tripping in the dark over Lego creations and stinky baseball shoes.

Next thing they knew, the kids would find themselves removed from their cozy beds and spending the next fifteen minutes under the direction of drill-sergeant momma, turning the chaos into something bearable—all accompanied by a tongue lashing, of course.

When my husband gently pointed out that this was not an ideal way to spend the last half hour of the day, I realized I needed a better plan. First I started having my children straighten their bedrooms at least once during the day. Then I vowed to end the bedtime-cleaning rampages.

Now if the room looks like a cyclone, I'll kick aside debris so that no one will trip on the way to the bathroom in the night and try my hardest to ignore the rest. Sometimes if the mess is really awful, I'll quietly tell kids they need to clean their rooms before breakfast. But I've stopped berating children about the state of their rooms right before they fall asleep at night. No kid needs the last words of the day from mom to be a lecture, no matter how well deserved. Better to brush the clutter aside and end the day on a positive note.

School Struggles: Other common struggles center around schoolwork. Almost all moms, whether homeschooling or public schooling, have spent time sitting next to a child at the dining room table, willing him to focus just long enough for them both to survive twenty problems of math.

Some of my children enjoy racing the clock. I'll say, "Let's see how many problems you can get done before the timer rings." One mega-mom gives wiggly children extra homework in the form of physical activity. For example, she'll assign nine jumping jacks, four toe touches, and two push-ups at the start of math time. She says that with the wiggles out, some kids are able to sit and concentrate much better.

She also offers what she calls focus incentives. She'll put a handful of M&M's on a plate in front of the child. After each math problem, the child is allowed to take a candy. This helps breaks up monotony and brings the child's focus back to the homework.

I find it easier to keep my cool when I am doing something else in the room. Often, children will do better when you are close by. In fact, sometimes children will signal that they need extra attention from mom by being extra needy at homework time. But that doesn't mean you have to sit looking over their shoulders, willing every pencil stroke. I'll start dinner or sit next to them with my laptop or I'll load the dishwasher. If I'm being productive while still remaining available, I find it much easier to keep my cool.

A huge key when dealing with poky homework-doers is to give children ownership of the problem. Make sure they know what they're supposed to do and remind them that nothing else is going to happen till this is done. Then leave them be.

Sometimes kids will need a session or two of staring at the problems till bedtime to decide to work. Sprinkle a bit of exercise in there even if the work isn't done. Chasing the dog around the yard for ten minutes is sometimes just the thing to break the logjam in the child's brain and motivate them to finish the work. But stick to your guns and require that the work get done.

Again, I'm not claiming I do this perfectly. Sometimes I still slip back into old habits, but when I preplan my reactions to the various stresses of the day, I spend much less of my life frustrated and biting back unkind words.

Oppositional Kids: Sometimes kids can go through spells when all they seem to want to do is argue. You say a movie was fun, and he says, "I didn't like it." You admire your daughter's hat, and she abruptly decides not to wear it. When kids get on an oppositional kick, it can get so exhausting that it is hard to know how to respond. The other day one of my daughters was having one of those days. I was getting ready to bake a pumpkin pie and thought she'd be pleased.

"No pie," she said, wrinkling her nose. "I want cake."

I was disappointed that she didn't seem pleased about the pie. She'd loved it the first time I'd made it. But with an effort, I decided not to take the bait and didn't say anything more than "hmm."

I was irritated. But after thinking over it, I realized we might just be able to turn that mood around. A little later, when she and I were out running errands, I said, "You know, if you want cake, you can make it yourself."

"Really?" she said, looking interested.

"Sure, what kind of cake do you like?"

We talked about the various kinds of cake she might make. When we got home, I walked her through the steps of baking a cake. She chattered delightedly as we worked, and she seemed to have a real sense of accomplishment when the cake turned out well.

I'm not always able to resist arguing with a kid wallowing in negativity. Often, I fall into the trap of thinking that I need to address rudeness or sassiness instantly. If I can remember to disengage when the negativity starts and take time to think about my response, I am almost always a more effective parent. Even a rebuke can be better heard when it is not spoken in the heat of the moment, and every now and then that extra bit of time to think gives birth to a really excellent solution.

For All of Us Who Aren't Supermoms

The most important thing to realize in this whole Supermom discussion is that parenting is just like any skill. The more you do it, the better you get at it. I didn't have the foggiest idea how to teach my children anything when they laid that first baby in my arms. But I learned—not perfectly, though. I'm still working on it. But don't think that you have to possess every parenting skill when you begin the job. Parenting provides lots of on-the-job training. Just keep plugging away and doing the best you can. Remember: kids were designed to be raised by humans.

PARENTHOOD AND STRESS

Will Bedtime Ever Come?

In the weeks after the birth of my first daughter, I spent my days in a fog of exhaustion as thick as cotton. I'd gone back to college when she was two weeks old, and I was studying furiously to graduate from nursing school in three months. Sleep deprivation was new to me. Parenting was new to me. My baby wanted to nurse constantly and wasn't yet sleeping more than an hour at a time.

One night my husband agreed to sleep out on the couch with her for a few hours and to give her a bottle if she needed it. Fantasizing about three hours of unbroken sleep, I sank into bed gratefully. Less than an hour later, I woke to the sound of her crying. I pulled the pillow over my head, thinking my husband would have the bottle ready in a minute and she'd quiet down soon. But on she cried, louder and more angrily by the minute. What on earth could be wrong? I stumbled out to the living room, eyes glazed. John snored on the couch like a Wild Kingdom rhino that had been tranquilizer-darted. Our daughter screamed in her car seat scant inches from his ear. As I leaned down to pick my enraged, red-faced little one up, I realized the binkie was stuck—stuck!—to her face.

I didn't have my contacts in and couldn't see clearly what had happened. I was afraid to tug too hard. Was the binkie defective? Had her lip gotten pinched in a crack in the plastic? Frantically, I tried to free my baby from her binkie. That's when I realized that the binkie was *taped* to her face.

Scotch-taped.

Though my daughter's screaming had not roused my snoring spouse, my swift punch in the shoulder did. He opened his eyes just in time to see his wild-eyed wife peeling the tape off the baby's face. No, she hadn't been harmed. Her skin was unblemished, and she was fine once she had her momma back and that dratted binkie was detached from her face. But I didn't get that unbroken three hours of sleep for at least a couple of weeks more. And I pretty much gave up on the idea that my husband might be able to share the care of our daughter at night.

Helping Kids Sleep Better

Listen in on any group of new moms and eventually the talk will turn to sleep: who's getting it, who isn't, and how to get more of it. Sleep is one of the pivotal issues to affect a mother's well-being, especially in her baby's first months home.

Everyone has an opinion on what works. The smug and fortunate moms of "sleepers" are almost certain to expound upon the way to get babies to sleep. But I am not convinced there is one right way for every child. Babies are different. They can tolerate different levels of noise. Some sleep incredibly lightly. Others need much more sleep. The same is true for parents. Some parents need nine hours of sleep a night. Others can sail through a day on five.

When talking about babies and sleep, the name that is most often heard is Ferber. People talking about "Ferberizing" their babies. That is, they put them to bed and let them cry for a few minutes, checking on them regularly. They gradually increase the time away until the child stops expecting the parent to respond at night. A friend of mine who is a mother of eight swears by this method. She says if you begin when a baby is only a couple of months old, they will quickly learn to sleep all night. She is a wonderful, in-tune mother, and she has some of the nicest kids I know. Obviously, this has worked for her.

I personally have not been able to tolerate the cry-it-out method with my children, even though I have tried it in desperation with a couple of them. Maybe I have a guilt complex, but when my babies cry, day or night, I want to help them stop. The approach that has felt most right to me is the one espoused by pediatrician (and father of many) Dr. William Sears. His is an attachment-parenting approach.

We co-sleep during the first year. I nurse or bottle-feed on demand and don't actively try to train kids till they're at least a year old or, in the case of an adopted child, till they've been home a year. I've found that sleeping with my babies gets us all the most sleep. A couple of my adopted kids were three before they would sleep alone all night, but my others were sleeping well on their own by the time they were fifteen to eighteen months of age.

Does being on call twenty-four hours a day get exhausting? You bet. But I personally feel best about myself as a mother when I respond to my children when they're distressed.

However, there is a third approach for parents who don't feel they're quite cut out for attachment parenting and co-sleeping, yet don't feel comfortable letting their children cry it out. Some folks get desperate on lack of sleep and very quickly want to help their babies hurry into better sleeping patterns.

There's a wonderful book called *The No-Cry Sleep Solution* by Elizabeth Pantley. She incorporates some aspects of active child training with a really nice sensitivity towards a child's needs. The concepts in her book work with both the normal needs of any child and the extra attachment needs of adopted children. Her solutions are not instant but have the potential over a few weeks to improve a baby's sleep. Her strategies focus on nurturing attachment while still giving parents some level of control over the sleep situation.

Coping with What You Get

All babies eventually outgrow night waking. But what do you do
in the meantime when weeks of wakeful nights can leave you feeling
like you're wading through molasses? When my kids were young
infants, I had weeks on end where I dreaded night. During the day,
you're supposed to be awake, after all. Good humor is easier to find. But
at night there's all that thwarted hope—hope that you'll get more than
an hour or two of sleep, hope that the baby will finally figure out this
sleep thing—mixed with an underlying fear that if you handle
this wrong, the kid may never figure this out.

One of my adopted children came home at the age of four months
but slept like a newborn for months. He woke up every hour and a half
until he was nine months old. We finally realized he had a milk allergy
and was having terrible bellyaches from the milk we were feeding him
at bedtime. No wonder he was miserable!

We cut cow's milk out of his diet, and the very next night, he slept
five hours straight for the first time ever. He continued to sleep four
or more hours a night from then on. It was incredible what a
difference it made to cut out the dairy in his diet. I wished I'd done
it months earlier.

But I learned something during those months. Every morning after
those terribly brief, ridiculously restless nights of sleep, I would wake
up thinking that today was certainly the day I was going to die from
lack of sleep. Seriously. Maybe it sounds silly, but I was so exhausted.
He was our fifth child, so you'd think I should have been used to sleep
deprivation by then. But he was exceptionally restless at night. And
with four other kids under the age of ten, I couldn't just spend the
day in bed catching up on my sleep, even if the baby had allowed it.

I had to function.

Somehow, incredibly, I did. No matter how tired I was, no matter
how gloomy I felt at the start of the day, I'd make it to the end of
each day and think, wow, I did it. I survived again. Sure, I was yawning.

Sure, I craved my bed. But I was functioning, and, each evening, I would be amazed at the miracle of it, because it was a miracle.

In the Bible, God says he watches over mothers. I believe that wholeheartedly. If you are struggling with sleep deprivation, I would urge you to pray each evening before you go to bed that whatever sleep you get will somehow be enough. Sure, you can pray that your little owl will sleep, but also pray specifically that God will make the sleep that you get be enough.

Another thing that may help is to consciously let go of ideas about sleep that you may have. Maybe you've always thought you must have seven hours of sleep or that a night is ruined if you wake more than twice. Let go of those notions. You may need to turn your clock away so you can't see it in the night. When you're awakened, don't bother to count the hours of sleep you have left or tally the number of times you've been awakened. Psych yourself to respond calmly to your child and go back to sleep as soon as you can.

Rejuvenation in the Thick of It

Getaways and errands alone and quiet times in the tub are lovely restorative things. But if we begin to think of escape as our only good way to recharge, we may be setting ourselves up for frustration. Sometimes, in the thick of mothering young children, there's no practical way to get away on a regular basis. We moms need to discover ways to rejuvenate our spirits in the midst of the action, in the heart of mothering. If we can do that, we have much more power over the direction our moods take.

Faith: When I feel my morale slipping, too often I try to grit my way through on good will and determination alone. But determination can only take you so far. If I remember in the morning to find time to read the Bible and pray for my most urgent needs, my day unfailingly goes better. The Psalms are a fabulous tool when your morale is as low as a baseball team on a losing streak. David understood depression. Reading about his struggle makes me feel less alone and always points me toward God, the only true source of strength in my life.

Music: Not long ago, I was the surprised and happy recipient of an iPod. That thing has been an amazing source of encouragement to me. My daughter and I are sharing it and have filled it with a mix of contemporary and traditional praise and worship songs. With the iPod in my pocket and encouraging music in my head, my mood stays steady even in the midst of a mess.

My kids appreciate the uplifting power of music as well. On exhausting days, when it feels like I've permanently lost my funny bone, I'll pop some kids' praise music into my CD player and blast it away while I work. Soon I am singing, and often I have a kid or two singing right along with me. Dancing helps too. Even if I feel like I am too tired and cranky to dance with my kids, when I do, I feel rejuvenated and more like the mom I really want to be.

Carrien is a mother of four children. She also tries to remember the power of music in her life:

> I sing happy songs. I sing songs with words that lift me out of the self-pitying fog I can lose myself in. I sing songs that restore my perspective. It works when I am tired and walking the floor with a sleepy baby. It works when I am picking up yet another Lego after I have stepped on it. It even works when I am exhausted and wish I could, just once, sleep until I am not tired anymore. Singing gets me through and helps me to be a better mom.

Fifteen Minutes Better: Recently, I was feeling drained by the demands of my life. Homeschooling five elementary-aged kids at once is no slouchy thing, especially when two of them are just learning English. Add a three-year-old and three teens to the mix, and it's no wonder I had been feeling frazzled. I was most frustrated with the way my to-do list was taking time away from my family. Each night, I would go to bed thinking that although many things had gotten done, I hadn't really focused enough on everyone.

I'd lie in bed trying to remember the last in-depth conversation I'd had with my teenaged sons. I'd feel bad because I'd forgotten once again to play a game with my three-year-old. I would manage to fit in the fun at times. But, overall, I feared that my drive to accomplish the work was sucking the fun out of our lives.

I'm a realist: as much as I'd love to spend all of every day on intimate connection with my children, things still have to get done. And yet I was convinced I could do better at fitting in the fun. I decided to spend a month focusing on improving just fifteen minutes of each day. This small bit of improvement seemed much more manageable to me than the lofty goal of being a better mom all day every day, and as I took time at the end of each day to journal the good things that I managed to squeeze in, I found that aiming at just fifteen minutes helped me maintain a better focus all day long.

The moments I wrote about were usually not huge. I had a tickle war with a couple of my children. I played cards with a kid who was cranky. I sat on my teenager's bed and asked him a few questions. I chose to forgive a kid instead of lecturing her. I stayed up late for a nice chat with my husband. I let my three-year-old "help" me clean my bathroom. I pulled out a craft on a quiet afternoon. I took the kids for a bike ride. I lit candles at dinnertime.

When you're feeling exhausted, it can be tempting to just coast along, doing the bare minimum. But I discovered something interesting during that month-long experiment. Over and over again, I'd find myself at bedtime, not thinking about what I'd checked off my to-do list, but smiling at the joy I'd found in those little "better" moments. Those were the best moments of the day for me and my children. Making time for the good stuff rejuvenated me and made me feel like a better mom.

Remember, activities don't have to be complicated—storybooks instead of a DVD player, play dough on the picnic table, or a tea party on the front lawn. Afterwards, let your kids wash the dishes in a dishpan on the grass.

When you're trying to escape your kids so you can catch a breath, they seem to sense it and get even more needy. But when you sit down and play, even for a few minutes, it relaxes and encourages your children.

Full disclosure here: play is not easy for me. I am a ridiculously task-oriented person. Sometimes I literally have to look at the clock and force myself to play for 15 minutes straight without wandering off. But I never regret disciplining myself in that way.

Carrien has also found her path to rejuvenation through reaching out to her little ones:

> I try to remember that my children are more important than paperwork, tax returns, insurance forms, laundry, dirty floors, and all of the other things I seem to be drowning in. It's easier to remember this if I sit down and spend time with them instead of treating them like flies buzzing around my head as I try to work, swatting them away in annoyance.
>
> I take up residence in a comfortable chair and get them to tell me stories. I read a few books to them, if I can stay awake long enough. I hug on purpose and store up Mommy kisses for the time later in the day when I need to concentrate on something else and need them to play quietly on their own. I try to remain open to my children.

Making Time for Your Marriage

Another source of rejuvenation during the hectic years of parenting many young children can be your relationship with your partner; that

When you're trying to escape your kids so you can catch
a breath, they seem to sense it and get even more needy.

is, if you can manage to make eye contact in the midst of multiple
children all clamoring for attention at once. Traditional wisdom suggests
a regular date night as key to a happy marriage. Date nights are
wonderful and restorative. Some couples even manage to coordinate an
overnight getaway once or twice a year.

But for most of us, times away only comprise tiny slices of life. It is
vital to find ways to connect that don't always involve arranging sitters
and packing bags for weekend getaways. Don't get me wrong—getaways
are lovely. But what you do with the many ordinary days in between is
much more important.

One thing that John and I like to do is sit on the porch in nice
weather after he gets home from work. Kids get a lovely burst of energy
playing outdoors in the evening just before bedtime. They know that
pajamas and toothbrushes are right around the corner, unless they get
on a really nice play jag that mom won't want to disturb. The fading
evening light seems to make bikes and basketballs and skates and
sidewalk chalk more interesting. As the light dims and the kids play,
John and I get a chance to chat about the day.

A friend of mine treasures the time she and her husband make to
talk about their lives:

> *Laughter has been an incredible "glue" that holds us together.
> We often will have an experience, then laugh together about
> it and say, "Let's remember this," and we do. We tell each other
> the same stories [repeatedly] over the years. Those stories
> have given us so many hours of joy and sharing/connecting.*
>
> *The late-night talks are probably the deepest and most
> heartfelt times of our marriage. We do not "schedule" these*

talks. Just sometimes, the hopes, dreams, worries, and fears come tumbling out, and we can listen and share for a long time in the comfort of the dark night in our bed, just us murmuring dreams and fears and knowing that we will always be there for each other.

Jenni in Fremont, California, also mentions the power of sharing special memories. She and her husband even created their own memory jar:

About five years ago, my husband gave me a memory jar for Valentine's Day. It was half-filled with handwritten memories from the years we had already spent together. Ever since then, we have been adding memories to that jar. Now that we have the kids, our memories have taken on a new dimension. When we spend time picking memories from the jar and reading through them, we can really see how much our relationship has grown and developed over the years. It's a nice activity that helps us to appreciate where we were, where we are now, and where we might be headed in the future.

My husband and I have a long history of letter writing. For awhile, when we were working opposite shifts, we had a notebook that we both wrote in, passing it back and forth between the two of us. These days, we don't write regularly, but if John knows I've had a hard day, he'll take time the next morning to write me a few lines of encouragement and leave the note on the bathroom counter so I'll find it first thing in the morning. In one of my bathroom drawers I have dozens of little notes he's written me over the years. On his side of the mirror right now is a lipstick heart that I put there just to make him smile.

A lot of our success, I think, hinges on the small stuff, the tiny daily actions that make a person feel loved: the way my husband puts that first cup of coffee in the morning right into my sleepy hands without me ever saying a word; making time for romance on a regular basis, even when we're tired; saying "you smell nice," when he does; hearing "you look beautiful," even when I feel frumpy; having a secret sign for "I think you're hot!"

Even a slice of watermelon can be significant. Our family can easily eat a large melon in a meal or two. I am in the habit of chopping the whole melon at once, laying quartered slabs in a huge bowl to serve at a meal or two till the melon is gone. But before I quit cutting, I set aside one perfect thick round on a plate, sticking a spoon in its center. John loves his melon in huge slabs, you see, and so I try to save him at least one piece of each melon to eat like this.

Equally important is the handling of the other little stuff—the not so good stuff. You know, the dirty socks lying on the floor right next to the hamper, the lost TV remotes, and the moments of snarling impatience where he (or I) have had it up to our eyes with something else and some of the nastiness spills over to each other. Everyone has moments of frustration. The trick is to mindfully choose to set aside those little irritations—to decide that they don't deserve to inhabit a large space in your mind.

My husband and I don't get it all right every day. But we do get some of it right most days. That's the beauty of being intentional about the little things. Let's face it, if your life is so frantically busy that you can't fit in something small like squeezing your hubby's rear as you run past him on the way to baseball practice or putting the paper down to look her in the eyes for two minutes while she talks to you, well, then, your whole life needs a little reworking.

Handle the little things right, and you'll find the bigger issues easier to resolve as well. So I'll keep slicing that melon just the way he likes it and be thankful each morning as he hands me that steaming cup of coffee. Some day we may even get to Hawaii. But until then, we are doing just fine.

HINTS FOR A NEW MOTHER

- If someone offers help, ask them to bring meals, run errands, scrub sinks, or fold laundry. Don't feel guilty about doing all the baby cuddling yourself. You are the momma.

- Don't stress if dad does things differently than you do. Kids benefit from both dad-style and mom-style parenting.

- Mothering, like any new skill, can be hard at first. But it will gradually feel more natural as you find your own style of doing things. Really.

- Sleeping with your baby is a great way for many moms to get more sleep and to get in some extra bonding time. It doesn't feel comfortable to everyone, but give it a shot. It may work for you, and when it works it is sheer bliss.

- Take a nap every day—for your sanity. Even twenty minutes while your baby sleeps can be very restorative.

- Take a walk every day—for your body and your mental clarity. Your baby will love getting out too.

- Have some chocolate every day—for medicinal purposes, of course.

- Remember, responding to your baby's cries is not spoiling her; it is nurturing her. Spoiling is something that happens to fruit when it is ignored too long, not to babies who are well loved.

- Trust your instincts! Many people will give you advice. Don't be afraid to listen to the bits that resonate with you and toss out the rest.

- Take one day at a time. You can do it! Motherhood is hard, but it is also one of the very best, most everlastingly meaningful things we can do to contribute to the future of our world.

PARENTING HACKS

Isn't There a Better Way to Do This?

The other evening, I sent the younger children off to the bathroom to brush their teeth before bed. When I heard screaming in the bathroom, I went to investigate, arriving just in time to see a drinking cup flying past my head. This provoked a stern lecture, during which the offender forgot to pay attention to the fluoride rinse he was pouring into his cup, which overflowed.

At that exact moment, his brother accidentally bumped his elbow, adding even more $3-per-pint liquid to the puddle already on the counter. As I reached for a towel, I spotted my three-year-old standing on a step stool at the sink blissfully washing her hands, drenching the front of her pajamas in the process. After peeling off her wet things and wiping up various puddles, I tossed laundry away, only to see that the thirteen-year-old had apparently not done any laundry that day.

I called in not-so-dulcet tones for him to complete his mission, and I went into the five-year-old's room to tuck her in, only to find several dozen stuffed animals, three games, and sixteen items of clothing all over the floor. The five-year-old swore up and down that the three-year-old was at fault. It was about then that I got a strident tone to my voice, and my husband hurried in to ask me why I was in a bad mood all of a sudden.

As parents, we all have moments like that, when the cumulative

The best way to encourage good behavior in grocery stores is to begin even before you walk through those big automatic doors.

effect of many little irritations takes us down. The difference with a large family is that there are so many more opportunities for this type of chaos. It is wise to expect a certain amount of craziness. But there are things we can do to minimize chaos in the craziest parts of the day. Whether you're serving dinner or shopping for groceries or tucking kids in at night, everything will go more smoothly if you have a plan.

Surviving the Grocery Store Gauntlet

I have a friend who says she'd rather gouge out her own eyes than take her four kids grocery shopping—and she's only half joking. Shopping with a horde of kids can be challenging. Some moms just leave the kids home with dad when it's time to run to the store. I often bring only a couple of kids at a time, leaving the rest in the care of a teenaged sibling. But what if you don't have that luxury?

Sharon Leonard, a mother of 11, says she routinely takes eight young children with her to the grocery store:

> I take them with me because they need to learn how to act
> in public, how to shop, and how to find bargains—they are
> good at it! Plus, I don't have a babysitter. When my husband
> comes home, I go to work. On rare occasions, I trek up to the
> twenty-four-hour Super Wal-Mart thirty minutes away at
> 2 a.m., but it is a bit lonely without the entire gang! They love
> to grocery shop.

Sharon makes a great point. Kids learn important skills when we take them out in public. But no mom wants to be that red-faced woman hissing orders through clenched teeth at sassy kids intent on dismantling the store. The best way to encourage good behavior in grocery stores is to begin even before you walk through those big automatic doors.

Make Expectations Clear

When we pull into the parking lot at the grocery store, I go over my expectations even before kids are out of their seats. Reminding kids of the rules sets the tone for the shopping trip and removes the "I didn't know that" excuse. Shopping rules are simple: respect people and respect property.

Respect People

Respecting people includes all interactions with anyone in the store. I remind my kids that they respect strangers by not running around corners and bumping into them, not blocking aisles, and not bellowing.

They show respect to mom by giving me enough space to look at things. Usually that means walking behind me instead of milling around right in front of me. It's a lot easier to compare the price of generic Cheerios to the name-brand ones if I don't have a wall of kids between the goods and me.

Respect extends to siblings as well. Some moms who've had trouble with kids fighting in the store have given their younger kids assigned corners of the shopping cart on which to hold while shopping. Though I don't do this routinely, I use this as a consequence if my kids seem unusually bent on mischief.

Respect Property

Respecting things involves not touching items that you don't intend to buy. If a child has trouble with this rule, he can walk with his hands in his pockets for an aisle or two. I also expect my kids to stay out of the clothing racks in clothing stores. Not only does it give mom heart failure when she can't locate a kid but it also tends to knock things off racks and onto the dirty floor.

One of the problems with shopping time is that kids seem to know moms have fewer discipline options available when out and about. It can be easy to feel like you just need to endure your way through the shopping trip so you can get home. But if you have a child who perpetually causes trouble in the store, you may need to simply walk out of the store and go home a time or two to be able to quickly assign the child a consequence. One mom I know even called a friend to come sit in the car in the parking lot with the child while she finished her shopping.

Occasionally, if the weather happens to be mild, I'll ask an older teen to sit in the car with a younger sibling. This buys me enough time to check out, and it also impresses upon the child the importance of obedience. Usually a child has to sit and wait in the car only once before concluding it is better to obey.

I remind my children that we are ambassadors wherever we go. We represent large families. We represent adoptive families. We represent homeschooling families. We can't expect our kids to behave perfectly all the time. They're children, after all, but communicating clearly with kids and having a plan in place for misbehavior increases the chance that they'll bring us happiness instead of headaches when we're out and about.

Let Kids Know What the Agenda Is

Respect goes both ways. Often, kids will want to spend money on a shopping trip. But some days, a fifteen-minute stop in the Lego aisle contemplating the virtues of a spaceship versus a race car will make mom late to pick up an older sibling from baseball practice. Whenever it's possible, I try to tell my kids before we get out of the car whether or not this trip is an allowance-spending trip. Sometimes I will also remind kids that the more helpful they are during the boring portion of the shopping trip, the more likely it is that we'll have time for the toy aisle.

Consider Older Kids' Feelings

I remember my feelings as a teen shopping with my family. I often felt self-conscious about the stares our large family got. Most of my big kids seem less appearance-oriented than I was as a teen, but I still try to keep their feelings in mind when we are out shopping.

Once my kids reach the age of ten or so, I will give them shopping assignments. I'll send a couple of kids across the store for the item located in a far corner, with instructions to meet me a few aisles ahead of where I am at the moment. I'll send a couple of others back an aisle or two to grab what I forgot to get there. Most of my kids are familiar with the brands that we buy and can pick out things fairly easily. Most of them also know to check the unit pricing when faced with two similar brands.

The kids enjoy these errands. It gives them practice shopping, and speed helps us get done more quickly as well. My teenage girls will often spend a few minutes browsing the clothing racks at Wal-Mart while I'm grocery shopping. Don't forget safety, though. I don't let my preschoolers out of sight, and I don't let kids wander the store without a sibling till they're teenagers.

The Gimmies

One irritating grocery store problem is begging. Decide what's tolerable to you, again keeping in mind that what is tolerable from one child may be downright crazy with five kids begging at once. You may see no problem allowing a child to select a pack of gum at the checkout at the end of the shopping trip. Or, with good behavior, you may decide to allow the child a few moments to spend some money. But if you'd rather not get into the treat-buying habit, tell your child your decision upfront and then stick to it. If begging is an ingrained habit, it may take awhile to extinguish. Most likely you will need to come prepared with some appropriate consequences for begging.

At first you may allow three warnings about begging (keep a running tally on the side of your grocery list). Later you may have a zero tolerance rule. One of the things I tell my kids is that misbehavior drains my energy. If they wear me out while we're out and about, they'll need to help me with my work once we get home.

Keeping Toddlers Gainfully Employed

The great thing about preschoolers is that they love to help. Recently, I wanted to clean my bathroom, and my three-year-old asked to help. I swept the bathroom floor and moved the rugs. Then I gave her a spray bottle and a wet rag so that she could scrub the floor. I fully expected that she'd wander off in three minutes flat. Instead, thanks to the wonders of Windex, she scrubbed and sprayed for a full half hour. She was in bliss. When the five-year-old came along and saw what the three-year-old "had" to do, she joined right in too.

Little children love to feel like the work they do is real. The closer their activities come to mimicking something real that you do, the more likely it will be that your child will be engaged. Kids will probably decide eventually that housework isn't all that fun. Enjoy those early years when they are so eager to help.

Even a two-year-old can peel a carrot with a little bit of instruction and a good peeler. Sometimes the carrot ends up all peel, but carrots are cheap and keeping a two-year-old occupied for twenty minutes is priceless.

A three-year-old can spend ten minutes buttering his own toast if you let him. A five-year-old will have a wonderful time washing her dolly's clothes in a basin on the back patio. Kids also love "painting" the steps or the siding on your house with a paintbrush and a bucket full of water.

Here's a great activity for a day when your kitchen floor needs a mopping. Give your child a dishpan full of water set on the opened door of your dishwasher, along with a little heap of sturdy dishes that need washing. Lay a towel on the floor so it doesn't get too slippery. After awhile you can trade the soapy water for rinse water and supply her with a dry towel.

Bedtime Battles

As my story at the start of the chapter demonstrated, bedtime can be challenging. It comes at low ebb in everyone's energy. Once again, a routine will help pull you through. If your spouse is around in the evening, this might be a really nice time for stories or bath time with dad. With large numbers of children, it can work well to have the older kids settled in doing something quiet with dad while mom focuses on putting the youngest children to sleep.

One huge sanity saver at our house is a bedtime for the kids that is at least an hour or two before your own. Lots of parents these days just let kids drop in front of the TV or head them off to bed when the parents go to bed. But it is very restorative for parents to have an hour or two of kid-free time in the evenings.

Older Children and Routine

Once you finally get teeth brushed, stories read, pajamas found, and a path cleared through the room to avoid breaking a leg at 3 a.m., everyone is usually pretty tired. The temptation can be to make those last bedtime minutes brief. I try, however, to hang out next to each child's bed for at least a couple of minutes to chat—usually about something fun happening the next day or some other plan for the future.

Usually at bedtime I'm as dry as an empty juice box. All I want to do is go sit on the couch with my husband, and yet my children chatter on. It helps me mentally to expect it to take at least half an hour to make the rounds of people's beds, giving hugs and talking for a few minutes. Kids often really open up during those last few minutes of the day, and a few more minutes of patience helps end the day on a much sweeter note.

We put our under-twelves to bed a little earlier than our teenagers. Our older children will sit up with us for awhile and watch the news. But even our teens head off to their rooms at least half an hour before we go ourselves. They don't have to actually go to bed then, but heading them off to their rooms a little earlier than our own bedtime gives us a cherished bit of alone time.

Toddler Training at Bedtime

I tend to be fairly relaxed about where our youngest children sleep at night. Our babies have always slept with us till they were a year or so old. Our adopted kids have slept with us for a little longer than that; after months of orphanage life, they needed a little extra time as the babies.

But, eventually, for every child there comes a time for him to learn to sleep in his own bed. Switching a two-year-old over to a big-kid bed can be a frustrating time. Inevitably, the dreaded jack-in-the-box phenomenon will occur. You get the child to bed, head out to the living room for some hubby time, and within five minutes you hear the padding of little feet in the hall. Around the corner comes the jammy-

Toddlers can also feel great reassurance sleeping with a sibling. Putting the two-year-old to bed right next to the six-year-old may be all it takes to get some children sleeping on their own at night.

clad two-year-old, doing his best to look winsome—or pitiful—depending on his bent. Sometimes I swear the kid beats me to the living room.

Now what?

Here's what I do: I stick the kid back in bed. Then I grab a book and a comfy pillow and camp myself outside the child's bedroom door. There I sit until the child gives up and goes to sleep. When he pops up, I'll stick him back quietly, firmly, and matter-of-factly—over and over, until he gets the idea that bed is the only option. Some of my most stubborn children have needed to be replaced a dozen times before they got the message.

Once we have established that they remain in bed when I put them there, I work on getting the child used to mom being away for a few minutes at a time. After I tuck him in and he seems relaxed, I will tell him I need to go run a load of laundry or use the bathroom and promise to come right back.

I keep my first trip away brief, coming back quickly to reassure him. In a few minutes, I'll leave for a little longer. Always I stay close. If he gets up, I replace him firmly and quietly. Gradually, over a week or so, I will increase my time away, so that he will eventually get used to falling asleep with me out of the room.

Usually, a couple weeks of this kind of training will get the child used to a different bed. When you meet with resistance, try to figure out whether it's stubbornness or true fear. Some kids are just extra stubborn, and you just have to persevere until they get the idea you are serious.

But maturity is also a factor. If a toddler is still exhibiting lots of fear after two weeks in his new bed, I may decide to give him another few months in with mom and dad to mature before trying the bed switch again. Toddlers can also feel great reassurance sleeping with a sibling. Putting the two-year-old to bed right next to the six-year-old may be all it takes to get some children sleeping on their own at night.

In working towards helping little children sleep at night, it helps to remember that they grow up fast. When parenting a houseful of preschoolers, it can seem like you'll never have your bedroom to yourself again. But once you have a child or two grow up, you realize just how fast it happens.

My husband and I have actually been less eager to get our younger children out of our bed. Awhile back, we got a toddler bed for our youngest daughter, who was two at the time. She was thrilled. With me sitting nearby, she went to sleep easily that first night. A couple of hours later, when John and I were getting ready for bed, my husband looked wistfully at the spot in our bed where she usually slept. When he went in to check on her, he discovered she'd fallen out of bed and was now curled up on the floor with her bum up in the air and her arms and legs tucked under her.

"That's it," he said. "She's coming back in with us."

After getting her settled in her usual spot in our bed, we grinned sheepishly at each other. "That looks better," John said. "I'm not ready to have her sleeping alone."

I felt exactly the same way. After all, she might be our last baby. Why rush this growing-up thing?

Food Wars

A friend once told me that when she was a little girl, she was so picky that her mother had to dye her mashed potatoes pink to coax her to eat them. I was incredulous. In my family we ate what we were offered and were mostly happy to get it—except for the occasional peas that my sister hid on the ledge underneath the table, leaving them to dry and rain down on the carpet when the table was bumped on vacuuming day.

Though most parents don't resort to red dye #4 to coax their kids to eat, many parents struggle to encourage their children to eat a varied diet. Many kids would live happily on chicken nuggets, goldfish crackers, and fruit snacks. Moms get tired of fighting the food wars. It can feel a lot easier to keep the freezer stocked with chicken nuggets than to argue over food.

I've noticed that kids in big families tend to be less picky. My theory is that this is related to sheer practicality. When you're feeding half a dozen kids, you'd go nuts trying to be a short order cook for each and every child. So you offer fewer choices, and kids learn to be more flexible. Here's another thing that moms of many know: kids almost never starve themselves, despite their parents' fears. If they're given a reasonable variety of food, they'll eat enough to live on. Really.

Nutrition isn't the only reason to encourage children to be good eaters. Kids who like only a few foods are crippled in a way. They become adults who worry about dinner invitations or trips outside of the United States simply because of worry over unfamiliar food. Moms do kids a great service by training them to be flexible. But how do you do it?

Variety is a key to raising healthy eaters. Don't give up if your kids seem to hate the first taste of new things. Some researchers have found that children need to try foods ten times to get used to a new taste; others say the magic number is closer to twenty. Except in the case of extreme (translate: gagging) aversion, we encourage a couple of bites of everything presented and then allow the child to finish out the meal with other healthy items they enjoy more. I usually offer at least a couple of different foods at every meal so that there are familiar options along with the new foods being offered.

A great way to encourage kids to try new food is to enlist their help in the kitchen. Even a four-year-old will enjoy thumbing through a colorful cookbook and helping you pick a new recipe to try. A second grader can help make the grocery list. A fifth grader is old enough to cook a meal with you close by to answer questions. Many parents assign older kids one day a week to plan and cook a meal. Something about cooking for themselves encourages kids to be brave.

If you have a real veggie-hater, try gardening. Paging through a seed catalog or browsing a seed display at a local feed store is great fun for kids. Even a corner of a flower bed is big enough for a few carrots or a tomato plant.

Another key to healthy eating is to keep snacks healthy. Kids who fill up with junk every couple of hours naturally are less interested in eating healthy food at mealtime. My teenaged daughters keep us well supplied in homemade cookies. We have something sweet for dessert every day or two. But afternoon snacks are usually bananas or carrots or leftover breakfast pancakes.

Since we have children born in Ethiopia and Korea, I have made an effort to learn to cook items from each of these cuisines. Nearly every week our menu includes Korean and Ethiopian food. Some of the food seemed strange to us at first. But now everyone enjoys at least something from both cuisines. Most of our children are willing to try new things without any trouble.

Not long ago we had the opportunity to eat at an Ethiopian restaurant in Portland. One of my sons was less than pleased with the idea of Ethiopian food for lunch. He was afraid he would find nothing he liked to eat. Much to his delight (and mine), he liked everything that was served. One of the really nice things about both Korean and Ethiopian food is that small servings of many things are offered at every meal. This variety increases the chance that kids will find something they enjoy.

Avoiding Mealtime Craziness

One of the things that grows along with a growing family is the mealtime clamor. Imagine "Please pass the salt," "May I please have the milk?" and "Are there any more rolls?" all repeated half a dozen or more times per meal. For awhile at our house, we were feeling lucky to get in one bite before the next request came.

Finally we decided to switch from family-style serving to buffet style. Instead of putting all the food on the table, we set it on the counter in a serving line. The line goes in age order, youngest to oldest. Bigger people are assigned to fill the two little ones' plates initially. But other than that, everyone serves themselves.

This one practice has made mealtime much more peaceful. An added bonus is that we actually have to get up to serve ourselves that little dab more. This doesn't stop my hungry boys for a minute. But it does make me think twice about taking that second serving.

Kids in Church

There are two theories about kids in church. The first is that church should be like play. Kids spend a few minutes in the main service with parents before being led off to a friend-filled classroom to play, sing, and do crafts. Our children do this type of thing during Sunday School. But in church, they stay with us.

Some people feel that having young children in church with them is so much work that they might as well stay home. Some Sundays can feel like that, especially when children are between ages one and three. But expecting children to be in church from a young age trains them better for the future.

Yes, children are bored at times. When kids are toddlers, I bring a bag of goodies to dole out bit by bit: Cheerios, tiny notepads, stickers, Hot Wheels, and tiny dolls. Sometimes I end up having to stand at the back of the church for awhile with a restless child, especially near the end of our hour and a quarter service. But most children can tolerate church quite well by the time they are three.

We are fortunate that all the parents at our church are working on training their toddlers to be at the service as a family. It is nice to be in the company of other families with the same goals. Our church is full of little ones. There's scuffling and occasional fussing, but we're in good company; and I personally think it is wonderful to see all the children worshipping with their families.

If you attend a church that automatically separates families during the worship service, you'll have to decide whether you'll go along with the tradition of that church or find a new one for your family. Kids certainly can learn to sit in church at an older age, but I think that children benefit from worshipping with their family right from the start.

One thing that has really helped our pre-readers enjoy church more is to teach them some favorite hymns at home. Choose simple hymns with repeated choruses. Even two-year-olds can quickly learn a simple chorus. I'm amazed at how often a newly learned song ends up being sung in church the next Sunday. I can't tell you how encouraging it is to hear even my little ones singing along happily. Often those hymns are the only things that snag their full attention during the entire church service.

Bedroom Cleaning

One of the things that moms everywhere struggle with is bedroom cleaning. Who should do it? How clean should it be? What do you do when a child is not motivated to keep it decent?

I think this is a case where it is wise to "major in the majors." I ask my younger kids to straighten their rooms once a day. *Straighten* may be the wrong word—basically, we are talking clearing a path between the bed and the door so that people can get to the bathroom in the night without bodily injury. Edges of bedrooms are usually cluttered during the week. Once a week either I or a teenage sibling will go into the little kids' rooms, pull junk out of corners to the center of the room, and help with or supervise the cleaning depending on ability.

Sometimes I will sit in the hall between the bedrooms with a book, or reading stories to the three-year-old, and just be there to guide the cleanup. When several kids are cleaning together, whatever you do, don't divide the room in half. That always leads to fights over boundaries and items mysteriously migrating from side to side. Instead, I assign categories. I tell one person to clean up books and clothes and another to clean up trash and toys. Once those four categories are taken care of, usually the room looks much better and I can give other specific instructions as needed; for example, refold those jeans, straighten the shoe shelf, dust off the dresser, etc.

I do not clean a room for a child capable of cleaning his own. That only teaches kids to think of mom as the maid. In my mind, any kid over four is capable. I hold them accountable to the standard that is acceptable to me, and I give younger kids plenty of supervision. But as I said above, my standard is fairly relaxed. Usually, if we dig out once a week and path-clear the rest of the time, I can live with it.

I give my teenagers even more leeway. I only ask them to clean their rooms when company is coming, and even then I don't really inspect. I've found that the shame factor usually kicks in, and they do a fairly decent job. However, their rooms are upstairs, out of my view for most of the day. If I had to walk past messy rooms every few hours, I think I'd have more trouble being that relaxed about their bedrooms.

One thing that really makes room cleaning easier is regular de-junking. Some families make a habit of giving away one item every time they bring something new home, to keep the clutter down. Shannon, a mother of four, discovered that sometimes mom's best efforts to de-clutter can be met with resistance from kids:

> *My children, bless 'em, have inherited their mother's tendency to hold onto everything! I'm mature enough (usually) to fight this tendency in myself. They're not. [Recently] there was a large box full of treasures that I thought they might actually*

want to keep. We went through the box, item by item, while they tried to convince me that their little lives would surely end if I threw any of this stuff away. The items included many, many Happy Meal toys that had never been played with since the moment they entered our house, a Hacky Sack devoid of its stuffing, Hot Wheels cars without tires, and a purple plastic ninja whose head had been chewed off by our dog.

"Mom!" the little darlings begged in chorus, "We LOVE this stuff! It's our fa-a-a-a-avorite!"

In a rare moment of inspired parenting, I made a deal with them. "You can keep each of these things, but you have to spend thirty minutes playing with that item, and that item alone, tomorrow."

There were looks of bewilderment all around, while they tried to imagine what they could do with a headless action figure for half an hour. "If it's fun enough to keep, it's fun enough to play with for thirty minutes," I explained.

And wonder of wonders, the whole box went into the trash without argument. Can it be that I've finally found a way to inspire them to throw things away?

Expect Chaos

I've got one final tip to share regarding parenting a large family. Obviously, mothering in general involves a certain amount of chaos. Whether you have one child or ten, there will be times when the nine-month-old flings oatmeal on the carpet or the three-year-old throws up in the night—three times—and the seven-year-old loses his shoes—again. But in a large family, the frequency with which this stuff happens can be overwhelming.

My advice? Expect chaos. The more fully you embrace the chaos factor, the happier you'll be as a mom.

Expect chaos. The more fully you embrace the chaos factor, the happier you'll be as a mom.

If you expect all the coats to explode from the coat closet two or three times a day between the months of September and April, there will be no need to gnash your teeth and wail when it happens. Just holler for everyone within earshot and tell them each to hang up four coats.

If you expect laundry to breed in an immoral fashion in every corner of every bedroom every day, you won't need to fall to your knees screaming at the discovery that you are once again six loads behind. Simply set the timer to run a load every hour all day and end the day with a laundry-folding party for everyone planning to wear clothing the next day.

If you expect muddy boot prints to adorn your floor even in the most arid weather, instead of tearing your clothing and calling for your smelling salts when it happens yet again, you can simply smile at the nearest barn-boot-wearing sweetie, hand him a mop, and say, "Go to it."

If you expect all visible chocolate in the house to be routinely devoured, there's no need to spend the baby's nap in a quivering heap of chocolate withdrawal. Simply tiptoe to the oatmeal bin and pull out your very own private stash of excellent chocolate to nibble surreptitiously. If you're feeling very charitable, you can also share with your teenaged daughters. Because, as my eight-year-old son once said, "Womans needs lots of chocolate."

Chaos happens. The key is to find ways to deal with it, and usually that involves making your kids take their fair share of the responsibility for the cleanup. After all, they made the mess.

LIKEABLE KIDS

Will Grandma Be Worn Out by Our Brood?

Nice kids. We all want them. We all have moments when we wish ours were a little nicer. No one has more reason to want nice kids than mothers of many. One kid whining is irritating. Two kids whining is more agonizing than fingernails on a chalkboard. Being surrounded by whiners is a fate you'd wish only on your worst enemy—or maybe your kids, just for a day, to pay them back for the miserable moments they've given you.

As families grow, parents tend to get more serious about child training. Part of it may simply be experience. Parents get more effective. But let's be honest here—part of this improved discipline is simple self-protection. A behavior that is tolerable from one child can make you crazy if done by three kids at once.

My husband and I only had two kids when we realized that the whining had to quit in our house. We made a serious push to stop rewarding that behavior. Though it didn't end entirely—we still fight the battle some days—it did diminish the level dramatically, which made my job as mom much more enjoyable.

Sometimes we can guilt-trip ourselves, fearing that we're only cracking down on an irritating behavior to make our own lives easier. But any lesson our kids learn about respect and polite negotiation will only help them out in life.

Awhile back I saw a clip from a TV news crew doing a ride-along

A behavior that is tolerable from one child can make you crazy if done by three kids at once.

with police officers who were trying to keep overly sauced St. Patrick's Day partiers off the road. A guy in a pickup truck was pulled over and his interaction with the police was caught on tape. Two officers approached the vehicle. After smelling alcohol on the man's breath, one officer asked him how much alcohol he'd had that evening.

"Nothin'," said the man. Never mind that the police officer was wincing at every breath.

Next the officer asked the man for his car keys. The man handed these over readily enough. He was not so thrilled when the officer asked him to step out of the vehicle.

"Wait a second!" he protested, alcohol fumes wafting through the air with every word. "First I need to know what you stopped me for."

The police reiterated their command, warning the man that he'd better obey. Still the man protested. Within two seconds those police officers had his door wrenched open, and him deposited neatly on his face on the asphalt, protesting in shock. Never have I seen a man exit a vehicle so fast, and headfirst too.

Unfortunately for him, drug paraphernalia fell out of the truck along with him. As if the alcohol on his breath wasn't damning enough. Next stop, jail. Just like that.

As I watched this scene on TV, I found myself thinking of my children. Sometimes when I ask my younger ones to do something, they swell like a puffer fish over the injustice of it.

"Why do I have to clean my room?"

"But I don't like to write essays!"

"I took a shower the other day!"

They huff in indignation over my audacious requests. My standard response to disrespect is to ask for a do-over. "Let's try that again," I'll say, and state my request again. They know by the warning on my face that this time I expect a respectful, "Yes, mom" instead of a belligerent, "Huh!?!"

Usually I get a better response the second time around. But sometimes I weary of fighting the disrespect battle. I feel like a mean mom, always riding someone. I start wondering if I'm expecting too much. Maybe a little sass is not such a huge deal if my children eventually get around to obeying.

The video clip shocked the sense right back into me. I don't ever want my children to be in the place of that foolish young man, disobeying the commands of a legitimate authority. I wondered if his mom took a lot of sass from him as a child. Maybe she never demanded respect.

Of course, I want my children to have discernment. Occasionally authorities abuse power and ask people to do the wrong thing. We've talked with our kids about avoiding abuse and not being weaklings who go along with just anyone. But in the case of legitimate authority, such as a teacher or a police officer or even good old mom, I want my kids' first response to be, "Yes, officer/ma'am/mom." There'll be time for questions (respectful ones) later.

Are We Raising a Generation of Obnoxious Kids?

Every team needs a leader. That applies to families too. Some parents are afraid of being overbearing. Others are negative about authority themselves. Those types of feelings can make it hard to feel comfortable being the leader. Walk through any store and chances are you'll run into at least one kid in passionate negotiation with a parent over junk he feels entitled to own. Some days it's my kid—our family is still a work in progress. But most of my children know that once dad or mom says no, it is time to drop the subject.

Is your home child-led or parent-led?

Is your home child-led or parent-led? A family with only a child or two may still function okay if the kids dictate most of the agenda. But the more children there are, the crazier it gets if the home is child-led. Often, it is the arrival of the third child that makes families suddenly realize that things have got to change.

Keys to Child Training

The very first key to happiness as a parent is to teach children to respect authority. Pick a few essential house rules and stick to them. Here are the rules we have at our house:

1. Be respectful to your parents.
2. Be kind to each other.
3. Work hard without complaining.

Sure, there are other, more specific things you'll need to address. But when you look at these rules carefully and think about the various behavior issues you have with your children, you'll see that the vast majority of problems are covered by these rules.

Once the child knows what behavior you expect, give consequences with every offense. Too often we parents think we are being merciful when we give kids one more chance to obey, but, really, we are training them to disobey.

Some parents fear that giving consequences on the first offense will doom them to doling out penalties forever. But once you decide to get serious, you'll be amazed at how quickly your kids realize it. Kids are smart, and they learn quickly when it is in their best interest. And here's the truth: learning to obey the first time you say it is in everyone's best interest. It makes for a happier family.

Effective Consequences

So what kinds of consequences are effective? Over the years, I've learned to vary the consequence depending on the occasion. If a child doesn't cooperate during work time, he'll need to work during part of his playtime. If a kid is cranky and argumentative, maybe he'd benefit from an earlier bedtime. If a child destroys his bedroom, he cleans up the mess. Kids who hurt siblings can make up for it by doing a chore for the hurt sibling.

Consequences should be meaningful, and, if possible, they should atone for the misbehavior. But you also should notice what seems most effective for each individual child. Some kids think it is a fate worse than death to go lie in bed for half an hour. Others would like nothing better. Some kids would be miserable without phone time for a week. Others wouldn't even notice.

Most kids do not like to do extra work. I will often give a disobedient child an extra job to atone for defiance. A five-year-old can spend five minutes mopping the kitchen floor with a wet rag. An eight-year-old might be asked to stack things more neatly in a cupboard. A twelve-year-old can wipe out the refrigerator. If kids learn that misbehavior takes away their free time, they'll be less likely to do the same thing again. I also find that getting a bit of assistance helps me feel more positive towards the child. If you are in need of some more inspiration regarding reasonable consequences, a great book is Foster Cline's *Parenting with Love and Logic*.

One thing that has helped our family greatly is a chart system called Champ Ladder (http://www.champladder.com). Over two decades of parenting, I've tried my share of star charts and reward systems. Many things seem to work for awhile, but I have a hard time remembering to keep using them. Kids seem to lose their motivation after awhile too.

This system allows you to customize ten different levels on the chart with rewards and consequences that suit your family and the ages of

*If kids learn that misbehavior takes
away their free time, they'll be less likely to
do the same thing again.*

your children. Kids earn various rewards such as computer time, TV time, and phone time. Their spot on the chart also determines their bedtime. On our family's chart, kids at level ten stay up till 10 p.m. Kids at level one go to bed at 8 p.m.

Kids earn their way either up or down on the chart depending on their behavior. If they get stickers for a day, meaning that they were generally cooperative during the morning, afternoon, and evening, they move up one level at bedtime. If they break house rules, they move down one level. At our house, sassing mom will move you down the chart—so will lying or hurting a sibling or disobeying an older sibling who has been left in charge. This means that one bout of disobedience moves you down one whole level on the chart, and it takes a whole day of excellent behavior to move back up.

This system works well for us. Kids are better behaved, and I am less frustrated. If someone is giving me grief, instead of lecturing or cajoling, I just go bump them down on the chart. There are also special reward cards you can use to move a kid up who is showing extra-great behavior.

When child training just seems too hard, remember you are giving your kids a gift they'll have for life. People who are respectful and hardworking and cheerful are more fun to be around. Employers these days complain about the difficulty of finding good workers. Too often people argue with the boss, complain behind his back, or simply wander off, leaving jobs half done. Teaching your children respect will make them stand out as adults in the job market.

"Yes, Mom!"

I have a friend with seven kids who was raised in the South. She asks her children to respond to her requests with a cheerful, "Yes, ma'am, I'll be glad to do it." The first time I heard her children say that, I was floored—and intrigued. As a mom struggling with the attitudes of my own children, those words were lovely to hear.

She explained to me that she believes that heart follows words. No, those kids don't always want to do what they are told. They're normal kids. Yet the requirement of a cheerful reply is teaching them what is right. Can you imagine how those children will stand out in the working world if they carry those types of willing words along with them?

After talking about it, my husband and I adapted her approach for our own family. We don't require quite as formal a response, but we do expect our kids to say, "Yes, Mom," or "Yes, Dad." Our teenagers, who have already learned to respond respectfully, can answer a little more casually. "Okay," or "Sure, Mom," is good enough for them, as long as it is followed by action.

If my children are having trouble coming up with cheery facial expressions to match their responses, I'll sometimes go stand in front of the mirror with them, so they can see just exactly how baleful they look. Usually, the sight of their own grumpy faces will provoke giggles. Then we can make silly faces at each other and talk about how different expressions look to other people: raised eyebrows versus lowered eyebrows, pursed lips or a relaxed mouth. Sometimes kids truly do not realize just how cranky they look.

If children are going through a stage where obedience seems unusually difficult, for awhile I'll ask them to say, "Yes, Mom, I'll be glad to do it." Of course, I would prefer that they be truly glad to obey and not just saying the words. But the point is to get them thinking about the response. With enough practice, hopefully right feelings will follow right actions.

Relationship building is another key to success in this area. We can't just dictate: we need to spend time doing fun things and hugging and touching and talking and showing love to our children. With the framework of cheerful obedience in place, the whole family is happier and more serene.

Once children know that obedience is a part of family life, then work on fine-tuning expectations for the various scenarios in which your children will find themselves. When parents take time to clearly communicate our expectations for various situations and let kids know what consequences might be for various misbehaviors, we dramatically cut back on the amount of misbehavior we'll deal with. That, in turn, leads to less stress and greater enjoyment of our children.

Job Training

Training children to help around the house is one of the central keys to success for a large family. Parents with only one or two children might be able to do all the housework themselves. But once you have four or five kids, the clutter, dishes, and laundry threaten to take over the world on a daily basis. Parents can't keep up with the mess that multiple children generate without help from the kids, nor should they have to.

But even more important, job training is life training. Unless you were born into a royal family, adulthood will include work. Kids need to learn to cook, clean house, and run the washing machine. Why not prepare our kids for reality?

Sometimes a false sense of guilt can keep a parent from training kids to work. Isn't housecleaning mom's work? Other times they are put off by the kid's response. A smart kid can put up so much resistance that it seems much easier to do it yourself. Preschoolers seem too young to help. Elementary-age kids are too tired after school. Teenagers are too busy studying. In my mind the teenage issue may be valid. But by the time the kids are teens, they should have years of experience helping.

The time factor plays into parent's decisions as well. We all know that the work will go faster if we do it ourselves. Why involve slow-moving, inefficient kids who are going to argue anyway?

This last barrier is very real, but only for the short term. When you are training kids in the five- to ten-year-old age group, yes, the work gets done slower and the quality often is not what you want it to be. But if you persevere in training and give them practice and inspect the work that they do, something wonderful happens after age ten or twelve. Gradually and steadily they get more competent, and you begin to reap the rewards for all that training.

Kids who spend their lives playing Xbox and IM'ing friends are not going to be prepared for reality: you know, the thing that happens when the trash is overflowing and the cupboards are empty and every piece of underwear in the house is dirty and there's no one but you to take care of these problems. Kids need time to play and enjoy life. But it is perfectly reasonable to expect them to contribute a little work to the family each day as well.

Job Training 101: Thomas Edison once said, "Opportunity is missed by most people because it is dressed in overalls and looks like work." By training our kids to work, we are making it more likely they will see those opportunities when they come along in life. Training should start young. Even a twelve-month-old can help put blocks into a bucket. Kids need to know that everyone in your family helps out, and they need to learn that complaining will not get them out of work. In fact, at our house, complaining is a great way to earn an extra task. Even an indignant "Uh!" means kids need to practice giving the right answer in the right tone of voice.

Don't just give children busywork. Kids are competent. A three-year-old can fold pants or towels. A seven-year-old can empty the dishwasher with the help of a step stool. Kids over ten can load the dishwasher, wash laundry, and clean bathrooms. It is better to overestimate your children's ability a bit and then train them to the task. Don't keep kids doing the same overly simplistic jobs for years. Promote them!

When you're training a child to do a new task, the best way to begin is by example. Break it down into a step-by-step process, demonstrating each step. Watch as they imitate you. Give them lots of praise and feedback; don't be afraid to show them a spot they missed, and ask them to redo something. Of course, you shouldn't be too nit-picky. Keep lessons short and cheerful. They are only children. But don't settle for laziness. You can tell if honest effort has been put out.

Training Tips: I remember sitting with one of my boys when he was five, training him to fold laundry. He was very resistant and kept lying down on the job—literally. Finally I told him that every time he stopped working I would toss a towel from the towel pile onto his pile to fold along with his clothes. It only took a couple of sessions like that for him to decide that it was better to work. The trick is to make obedience easier than disobedience.

To train kids to do more complex tasks, you may find it helpful to create a checklist. I remember being given the job of bathroom cleaning when I was a child. I struggled through the task for a few weeks, frustrated because my mother kept reminding me of all the details I hadn't done. Finally she wrote me a step-by-step bathroom-cleaning list. After that, I knew what her expectations were, and I didn't dread the job nearly as much.

If kids are having a hard time getting motivated, set a timer and give rewards for beating the clock. You can also have kids work on a larger task for a set amount of time each day until it is done. For some jobs, though, it works better to focus on the amount accomplished than the time spent.

We try to get out to the garden two or three times a week to weed. For awhile I'd tell the kids to each weed for half an hour. But with some of the less motivated (younger) children, much time would be wasted, and not much work would happen. I discovered that a much better way to motivate them was to hand them an empty ice cream bucket and tell them they could quit weeding as soon as their bucket was full to the top. Instead of teaching kids just to do their time, goals like these tend to motivate harder work and put kids in control of their own destinies. The harder they work, the quicker they can move on to fun.

One final, essential part of training children to work is to always inspect the work they've done. Always. Even young teens need the accountability of knowing that mom is actually going to look over their work. Be sure to give extravagant praise for a job well done.

Work alongside your children whenever you can. Have a preschooler hold the dustpan while you sweep. Fold towels with him. Gather several children and have a potato-peeling party. The more you can work together, the more pleasant it will be for the children. In fact, working together is a great way to bond. Suzanne Chandler says that when she is cleaning the kitchen with her son, she tries to remember that her first job is to build a relationship with him. Her second job is to train him in how to clean the kitchen. Her third job is to clean the kitchen. With an emphasis like that, job training is sure to be a success.

Division of Labor

When you're thinking about dividing up the chores in your home, it can sometimes be hard to figure out what tasks are reasonable for various ages of children. I began by deciding on the most important jobs that keep our home functional. For me, this list includes cleaning the kitchen after every meal, doing three loads of laundry each day, and cleaning and vacuuming the living room once a day. Various other jobs are done once or twice a week as well, but if the three core things are taken care of, then our home functions pretty well.

Age 3: Our three-year-old has an easy life. Her jobs include picking up her own toys, folding her pants on laundry day, and emptying the silverware rack every time the dishwasher needs emptied, usually two to three times a day. She is also my chief peeler. Any time a carrot or a potato needs to be peeled, she is my girl.

Age 5: The five-year-old clears the table after every meal. People clear their own plates, so basically she removes stray napkins and any odds and ends that are left and then wipes the table. She also cleans up her own toys and cleans her room with assistance. On laundry day, she folds her own clothes and someone else puts them away for her. She also empties the bathroom trash every day and vacuums the stairs once a week.

Age 9: Our two nine-year-old boys empty the trash on trash day and bring the cans to the road. They each empty the dishwasher once a day. They straighten the family room every day. They each do one load of laundry per day: sort clothes from the dryer in baskets, move things from washer to dryer, and put another load in the wash. On Wednesdays and Saturdays, they fold their own clothes, and fold and put away kitchen towels and bedding. Once a week, they clean their own room. Once a week, they work together to clean the bathroom that they use.

Age 10: Our ten-year-old daughter sweeps the kitchen every morning. She empties the dishwasher once a day. She helps the twelve-year-old wash pots and pans after the evening meal, since that meal tends to have the most dishes. Twice a week, she folds her own clothes, and folds and puts away bath towels.

Age 12: Our twelve-year-old daughter cleans and vacuums the living room once a day, and cleans her room once a week. She washes pots and pans after the evening meal. She folds and puts away her own clothes. She and the ten-year-old work together to clean their bathroom once a week.

Age 13: Our thirteen-year-old son does one load of laundry each day. Twice a week, he folds and puts away his own laundry, and is in charge of training the three-year-old to fold her laundry. He cleans the kitchen after lunch every day and mops the kitchen every Thursday.

Age 16: Our sixteen-year-old son does one load of laundry each day. Twice a week, he folds and puts away his own laundry, and also helps the five-year-old put away her laundry. He cleans the kitchen after breakfast every day and mops the kitchen every Monday. He feeds and waters the cow every morning. He also waters the plants and dusts for me every week.

Age 17: Since our seventeen-year-old is heading off to college soon and is taking some college classes during her senior year, we are gradually phasing her out of doing housework. This gives her more study time and will hopefully make it easier for us when she actually goes. She folds her own laundry and matches socks twice a week—a formidable task indeed in a house of twelve people! She also cleans the kitchen after dinner.

This system is working pretty well for us right now. At the start of each school year, I reevaluate the list, promoting kids to more challenging jobs as they are able. In addition to the above jobs, I assign two or three additional jobs to each child every Saturday morning. When most of my children were preschoolers, we were on maintenance. As they've gotten older and more capable, I have been able to add a few nice-but-not-essential jobs to the weekly list, such as dusting, cleaning the ceiling fan, and straightening the pantry.

All our kids are learning to be efficient workers—after all, the faster you get your work done, the faster you can play. By age twelve or so, my kids have learned most of the chores essential to running a home. They get plenty of playtime too. Skating, biking, playing video games, playing soccer, and climbing trees happen at our house on a near-daily basis. Because of this early job training, I am confident that our children will be well prepared for the working world. Their assistance also plays a huge part in keeping our home running smoothly.

Don't Forget Relationship

Though I've been talking a lot about teaching kids obedience, there is another part to this equation. James Dobson says, "Rules without relationship equals rebellion." Your kids will obey from their hearts only if your relationship is strong. Spend time every day on fun. Give lots of hugs. Praise them when you see them working hard at making good choices. Have tickle wars. Play board games. Build with Legos. Sing songs, cook together, be silly, dance, or go for a walk together. The better your relationship, the more your child will want to please you and the more fun you'll have together as a family.

Respectful Disagreement

Balance is an important concept to remember when we're training our kids. Yes, we want them to answer us respectfully and to obey cheerfully. But we aren't raising robots. Kids have feelings and opinions that they should be able to voice. You shouldn't have to listen to endless arguments every time your nine-year-old objects to cleaning out the guinea pig cage. Kids should be taught respectful ways to express themselves. We teach them not only to make our own lives more pleasant but also to give our children tools for the future—tools that will give them courage to speak when a coworker suggests doing something that is not ethical, or allow them to approach a boss who needs to hear another side of the story.

Consider the age of the child. Preschoolers, in general, don't have the discernment to be taught respectful disagreement. First they need

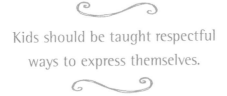

Kids should be taught respectful
ways to express themselves.

to master obedience. Once kids get into the early elementary years, we can start talking with them about ways to speak up when things are not going their way and about ways to approach different people.

A disagreement with a friend is handled in a different way than one with a teacher. A child can feel free to state his mind with a friend. If a child is in disagreement with mom or a teacher, he needs to first give a respectful answer. Only then can he respectfully state his reservations. If the person in authority is moved by one respectful request, that's great. If not, the child needs to accept the decision of the person in authority and move on to obey.

Too many parents allow endless argument in the name of allowing a child self-expression. That is exhausting to you as the parent, and let me tell you, it is not going to make any points with your child's boss later either.

If your older child feels strongly about something but is struggling to be respectful, try asking him to write out his argument. Most likely, the process of writing will help the child distill his argument to the core points, give him a chance to calm down, and give you something concrete to look at so that you can reconsider your stance.

Dealing with Lying

"Liar, liar, pants on fire," goes the childhood chant. If you've been a parent for any length of time, chances are you've caught your child in a lie or two. Experts say that lies told by two- and three-year-olds are just wishful thinking. Your child wishes she could tell you that she picked up her blocks, and so she says she did, in hopes that saying so will make it true.

There may be something to that wishful-thinking theory. But I've also seen preschoolers lie purposefully. Usually, if a child is doing the latter, you will see uneasiness, whereas a child involved in wishful thinking will tell the lie very cheerfully.

Lying can bloom during the elementary years if you let it. One thing to keep in mind is that lying is often a sign of fear. So how do you address that fear? Remind kids often that you'll always love them, no matter what. Reward truth telling, even if that means biting your tongue over broken china. I tell my kids that they'll end up in more trouble for lying about a broken glass than they will for actually breaking the glass. Accidents happen, and I don't always keep my cool. But I try to respond as steadily and predictably as possible.

Breaking the Habit: If I know that a child is struggling with truth telling, I give the child fewer chances to lie. If I see someone slugging her big brother, I don't ask, "Did you hit him?" Instead, I tell her to apologize and ask her what act of service she is going to do to make up for it. If the child protests and I sense a denial of the obvious coming on, I'll say, "Wait a second . . . only let truth out of your mouth."

Along those same lines, instead of saying, "Did you clean your room?" I'll ask the child if he is ready for inspection. In my experience, if fear is not the root of a lie, laziness often is. It's just much easier to tell your mom you've weeded the flower bed than it is to actually do the weeding.

Attitude of Gratitude

When I was a child, trying to choke down my liver and onions, I remember my mother telling me that children in Africa would be glad for that food. At that point, all I needed to solve that problem was a UPS box! But now that I am a mom myself, I understand the intent behind my mother's words. She wanted me to see my blessing.

Too many kids in America think they are entitled to everything: the newest styles, the coolest games, the most expensive bikes. It is an ugly thing. This type of attitude, grown up, manifests itself in adults who feel like name brands, new furniture, and exotic trips are their right in life, so much so that they will go into massive debt to supply themselves with the best. Forget helping out others: they think only about themselves.

Growing up in a large family teaches children a different viewpoint. Because many large families live on budgets, kids don't always expect the newest and the best. They know that others have needs too. They value what they have and feel fortunate when good things come to them. Some parents worry that they are somehow depriving their kids by not always giving them everything they request. Being raised in a large family teaches kids a healthier, more realistic view on life. All over the world, resources are scarce. Is it really right for kids to think they're entitled to their every whim when so many on this earth have so little?

Our teens have gained a more global view of the world by traveling with me to Korea and Ethiopia for adoption trips. Ethiopia is an especially eye-opening experience. Images of five-year-olds running alongside cars and begging are hard to shake. And that is a good thing. I passionately believe that in this world, we are responsible for more than ourselves, and I pray that my children will grow up with a heart for others as well.

Time invested in teaching our children to be respectful, faithful, hardworking, and caring is time that will pay rich dividends in the future. Sometimes we as parents can grow weary of the effort it takes to instill these qualities in our children. But we need to keep at it. These assets are at the heart of raising likeable kids—and happy, hardworking adults.

SCHOOL SUCCESS

What If My Kid Isn't an Honor Student?

Talk about education in a diverse group of parents and you may find yourself dodging sniper attacks. Public school parents see homeschoolers as overprotective recluses. Private school families think the public schoolers are risking their children's moral development. Homeschoolers see test scores as undeniable proof that everyone should homeschool. And, too often, when a parent speaks up to explain his or her own choice, people who've made other choices feel attacked.

For this reason, I want to begin this chapter with a disclaimer. I am a homeschooling mom. I think homeschooling offers many benefits to children, and later in this chapter I'll go into some of those benefits. But this chapter is about helping our kids succeed, no matter what educational choices we choose to make.

When I think of the young adults that I most admire in our church, I realize that they come from all kinds of educational backgrounds. All are strong, kind, moral hard workers—the kind of kids we all strive to raise. It is not their education they have in common. What they have in common is involved and caring parents. Parents who have taught them right from wrong—the kind of parents we all can be, whether we choose homeschool, public school, or something in between.

The Right Kind of Praise

One of the best things we can give our kids is the right kind of praise. Words of affirmation come naturally to many parents these days. A recent study by the University of Columbia found that 85 percent of parents believe that it's important to tell their kids that they're smart. The problem is that kids get used to being applauded for the simplest things. A parent will watch a child spend two minutes on a drawing and say she is a great artist. A kid who just completed a four-piece puzzle will be told he is so smart. Or a child who's just done a pounding rendition of "Mary Had a Little Lamb" will be declared the next Beethoven.

On the face of it, these bits of encouragement seem harmless and even kind. Certainly we should praise our kids. But remember that when your child gets into the broader world, eventually he'll meet a kid who can run faster or who can draw better or who gets higher math scores, and he'll start to doubt mom and dad's assessments of him.

Rather than giving huge applause for every action, it is better to praise specifics and to match the level of praise to the amount of effort that the child made.

"You really worked a long time on that puzzle!"

"I was so happy to see how kind you were to the new girl in your dance class."

"Wow, you practiced that song for twenty minutes! You really got better at it."

"Thanks for being patient with your little brother when he was grumpy today."

"Look at how shiny you made the kitchen floor! That took some real muscles."

"I'm proud of how long you worked on that multiplication! That takes perseverance!"

In the case of your budding artist, sure, comment on something you like about the two-minute drawing. Then maybe encourage him to add some more detail or talk about ideas for his next drawing. The most powerful praise focuses on things that children can control. We should notice effort. We should notice concentration. We should especially notice when kids have worked hard on a project.

In the end, hard work will get kids farther than native ability anyway. We can't all be the next Edison, but we can all learn to work hard. In fact, it was Edison who said that genius is 1 percent inspiration and 99 percent perspiration. Let's teach our kids the joy of really working at something.

A "Smart" Home

The second thing we can give our kids is a smart home environment. Computers and world maps and periodic tables taped to the walls are fine. But I am convinced that the very best educational gift we can give our children is a love of books.

Start reading to kids when they are toddlers, just a few minutes every day. Talk about the pictures. Have them point to objects. Continue to read to your children when they are older. Pick books that are a grade level or two above their own reading ability and spend fifteen to thirty minutes reading to your child each day. Talk with them about what you're reading. Ask them what they'd do if they were in a similar situation.

The Importance of Reading

John and I have always enjoyed reading to our children. We've read classic children's books like the Little House series and the Narnia series. We've read Bible storybooks, children's history books, and heaps and heaps of children's picture books. It is not uncommon for us to come away from the library with three-dozen books.

When we only had three or four children of similar ages, story time

FAVORITE READ-ALOUD BOOKS

Preschool Books
- *The Jesus Storybook Bible* (Sally Lloyd-Jones)
- *Tanka Tanka Skunk!* (Steve Webb)
- *The Napping House* (Audrey Wood)
- *Rolie Polie Olie* (William Joyce)
- *You Are My I Love You* (Maryann Cusimano)
- *The Sea Chest* (Toni Buzzeo)
- *The Day Jimmy's Boa Ate the Wash* (Trinka Noble)

Chapter Books
- Narnia series (C. S. Lewis)
- Little House on the Prairie series (Laura Ingalls Wilder)
- *The Phantom Tollbooth* (Norton Juster and Jules Feiffer)
- Childhood of Famous Americans series (various authors)
- *Trumpet of the Swan* (E. B. White)
- *Swiss Family Robinson* (Johann Wyss)
- *Caddie Woodlawn* (Carol Ryrie Brink)
- Junie B. Jones series (Barbara Park and Denise Brunkus)

simply involved gathering everyone up. But when your kids' ages range from babies to teens, reading time can get more complicated. Older kids may be bored by younger children's stories, and younger ones are not mature enough to understand the books directed at older children.

At the writing of this chapter, our kids at home range in age from three to eighteen. Currently, we gather everyone together in the evening at the younger children's bedtime. The teenagers bring their own reading books to read while my husband reads to the younger kids. First he does a short devotion, usually a story out of a kids' Bible. A current favorite of ours is *The Jesus Storybook Bible* by Sally Lloyd Jones. Then he reads a few picture books geared towards the youngest kids. Finally he reads a chapter or two out of whichever big book he is currently reading to the older kids at bedtime.

Usually story time lasts at least twenty to thirty minutes. Toddlers have widely varying abilities to sit through story time. Some can make it through half a dozen stories. Our current youngest (age three) gets twitchy after one or two and needs help from mom—and toys—to stay quiet the rest of the time. If she's particularly tired, I'll just take her to bed. But overall, story time is very much enjoyed at our house.

Since we are a homeschooling family, we are able to read during the day as well. Currently, I am reading the Little House series to the kids at lunch time. Sometimes I read while they eat and then enjoy my own lunch a few minutes later.

Other times I gather everyone in the living room right after lunch, hand out markers and blank paper, and read away. We've found that kids are less twitchy if they have something to do, and drawing doesn't seem to affect their ability to listen. Reading to kids even after they can read for themselves really helps stretch their vocabulary, especially if you choose a book just a little beyond what they can read alone and explain words that are more difficult.

Discover Their Learning Styles

Another way to boost your parental effectiveness is to discover each child's learning style. Whether you choose homeschool, public school, or something in between, schoolwork can take time. Figuring out the most effective tools to help each child learn will be worth every minute of time you invest. There are three basic learning styles: the auditory learner, the visual learner, and the kinesthetic learner. You can find more details about these styles at http://www.sdc.uwo.ca/learning/index.html?styles.

The Auditory Learner: The auditory person learns best by listening to directions and taking notes from speeches. He likes talking on the phone, sounds out words phonetically, and does a great job remembering verbal directions. When you're teaching an auditory child to read, he will often cue in more to your verbal "hints" than to the actual words on the page. Auditory kids often discover that muttering under their breath as they read boosts their reading comprehension. In fact, when one of my auditory children is stumped by a math problem, I will often ask the child to read the problem to me out loud. Often, just hearing the words is enough to help the child figure out the solution.

The Visual Learner: This person loves books, charts, and pictures. I'm a visual person myself. If you try reading me the directions for some new do-hicky, you'll have that book snatched out of your hand in ten seconds. I much prefer to read the directions to myself. Words make more sense when they enter my brain through my eyes instead of my ears.

When it comes to learning math, visual kids will often be able to figure out a tough story problem if you can just figure out a way to illustrate the problem. Visual kids naturally tend to be successful at school since so much of school is visually oriented.

The Kinesthetic Learner: The kinesthetic person is the original hands-on kind of guy. (And yes, he often is a boy.) He learns by doing. He gestures while speaking and uses lively expressive language. If you dare to bring him into a gift shop, you'll probably be wishing for handcuffs within two minutes.

Kinesthetic kids are the movers and the shakers. They tend to be least happy in a traditional classroom, simply because the demands of holding still and being quiet are too great. Kinesthetic people don't believe in reading directions. They prefer to plunge right in and get busy with their hands.

Figuring Out Your Child

Figuring out a child's dominant learning style involves observation and listening. Often, the words a person chooses will clue you in. An auditory person will include lots of sound words in his or her speech: I hear you. That sounds great. Listen to those seagulls!

A visual person's speech will be full of references to sight: I see what you mean. That looks great. Do you see what I'm saying? Look at that sunset!

A kinesthetic person, when he pauses long enough to talk, will likely prefer action words: Get a grip. I can handle it. Let's roll. Let me try it.

It is not always easy to figure out a preschooler's learning style. But once your child reaches elementary school, you'll be able to observe and give an educated guess about what works for him or her. A great resource in figuring out your child is *The Way They Learn* by Cynthia Tobias.

If you're not quite sure what works best for your child, do what savvy classroom teachers do: teach one lesson in a variety of learning styles. Multiplication tables can be a stumbling block for many second and third graders, but there are so many ways to teach them. Visual kids learn them well through flash cards. Auditory learners will enjoy CDs with multiplication songs. Kinesthetic kids will love playing "hop math."

Hop math is somewhat like hopscotch. Go outside and draw a hopscotch grid, arranging the numbers to look like the numbers on a calculator. Kids jump from number to number as they say the math facts.

The beauty of hop math is that it engages all types of learners, not just the kinesthetic types. The visual child sees the numbers. The auditory child says the numbers. The kinesthetic child moves her body from number to number. Once you figure out your children's learning styles, you'll be able to figure out ways to reach each of your little learners much more effectively.

Staying Involved in Your Children's Education

Whether they go to public school, private school, or homeschool, successful students tend to have one thing in common: involved parents. Most caring moms want to be active in their children's schools. But how do you make a regular appearance in three or four different classrooms when you are also juggling preschoolers? How do you volunteer for field trips? And what about all those darned fund-raisers?

First of all, find out which volunteer opportunities allow little ones to tag along. Holiday parties are often a good option since they happen infrequently. You can sign up just for the Valentine's party, for example, and there's usually no problem with bringing preschoolers along on party days. Recess duty is another good option. Preschoolers can play with the "big" kids, and the baby can ride in a sling while mom does playground duty.

You'll learn through experience what you can handle and what you don't have energy for. Shari, a mother of four, has learned what works best for her family:

> I don't volunteer directly in the classroom but will make phone calls, bake cookies, or donate items (used books, etc.)—things that I can do from home. The older kids help out at my younger child's school. At the carnival, my seventeen-year-old sold raffle tickets at one of the booths, leaving me free to hang out with my ten-year-old. I think having me with him was more important to him then me doing the volunteering.
>
> I do not sell fund-raising items ever—not for the schools, not for their sports organizations. I write a check to the school in lieu of fund-raising. I realize that is not an option for a lot of families, but it is what works for us.

Many busy moms also discover the importance of having a network of friends. Some moms trade child care so that each mom can have time to volunteer in children's classrooms. Others, like Lana, have found that working on a big project together can be an excellent solution:

> *One year, several friends and I, all with younger kids at home, put on the school carnival. We were the committee, so we met at each other's homes. Sometimes we'd bring the kids with us in backpacks, in strollers, or walking with us. When there was work to do, one would keep all the kiddos and the rest of us would do the work.*

Organizing paperwork is essential. You may want to set up folders or some type of mail slot for each child's paperwork so that you can keep track of permission slips and homework assignments. Preparing for school the night before is also a sanity saver. Make sure kids' clothes are picked out, right down to shoes and hair clips. Pack the backpacks, make the lunches, and do everything else you can possibly do to minimize the last-minute stress as you're walking out the door in the morning.

Finally, LeeAnn touches on one of the most important points of the school equation:

> *I have discovered that it's okay to let others know when you are overwhelmed, and to say no. When I let others know that I'm struggling to keep my head above water, the response is not criticism, but rather offers of help. Take advantage of those offers! Don't worry—the time will come when you're the one who seems to have it all together and you can return the favor to someone else who's drowning in carpools, science projects, and soccer practice!*

What about Homeschooling?

When our oldest three children were preschoolers, I never thought I'd be a homeschooling mom. I felt confident they could get a good education at our local Christian school. Our oldest daughter had a great experience during kindergarten. She was one of only eleven students. The teacher was great, and school only lasted half a day.

First grade was different. That loud busy class of twenty-four kids contained four children who spent the days bouncing off the walls and taking every minute of the frazzled teacher's time. The children like my daughter, who could sit still and did not demand attention, basically did not get attention. Amanda came home from school telling me she had to stay in at recess to finish her math because it was too noisy during work time. When I spent time in the classroom, I could see why. Even I would have had a hard time focusing in that level of noise.

What about Social Skills?

In the early 1990s, when we were first considering homeschooling, I had a lot of stereotypes (denim jumpers? head coverings? antisocial kids?) floating around in my head. But there was a woman whose family drew me in and made me curious. She had ten children—this was back before I ever dreamed I'd have ten myself! The teenagers in that family were the nicest teenagers I'd ever met. I knew that those were the kind of teenagers I wanted some day.

I asked this mom all the normal questions, including the one that homeschooling families are asked again and again: what about socialization? She shared a viewpoint I'd never considered before. She pointed out that children in traditional school settings spend lots of time interacting with other children who are as immature as they are. They learn ways of dressing, ways of talking, opinions about learning, and viewpoints on all sorts of important moral issues from friends—kids who are no older than they are.

In a homeschool setting, kids spend much of their time interacting with adults—and not just any adults—their own parents, the people who care most deeply about their success in life. Homeschooled kids seem more mature because they've had more opportunity to learn from adult behavior. It is adults who are eventually going to point our children towards being responsible adults themselves.

The "valuable" socialization that we tend to think kids are getting while surrounded by other children is often no more than a lesson in mass foolishness. Certainly, a dedicated teacher can do much to guide a large group of children in the right direction. But the children are also being hugely—and often negatively—influenced by the children around them.

It is essential that we as parents understand the tremendous power these other children will have on our own kids. We need to talk with our children about traits of a good friend, about the power of peer pressure, and to steer them towards kids who will influence them in positive directions.

We can even role-play what to do in tough situations. What if a kid is being picked on? What if your child is being mocked for what he believes? What if friends are trying to steer your child to do something wrong? If we give our kids tools to deal with these inevitable situations, we are making them strong, and we are also extending our (adult) influence beyond the times that we can be with them.

Do You Have to Be a Trained Teacher?

The next most common question concerns the credentials necessary to teach children. You do not have to be a teacher. You don't even need to have a college degree to be an effective teacher. You need to be motivated to help your child learn, and that is something that almost all parents considering homeschooling already are.

You don't have to know algebra or chemistry to teach your kids. There are lots of options to explore when your kids get to high school age and have tougher subjects. I opted to team-teach some science classes with a friend. Other families enroll their kids in enrichment classes available through the homeschooling community in many areas. Some families hire a college student to tutor their children. Other families buy online or DVD science and math courses that step kids through a workbook. Some programs even grade tests and offer help online and over the phone.

What about Testing? What about College?

Another concern surrounds the educational requirements of homeschooling. States differ widely regarding the amount of documentation required of homeschooling families. To learn about regulations in your state, visit http://www.hslda.org/laws/. We are fortunate to live in Idaho, a state where nothing is required of homeschooling families. Other states require extensive lesson planning and standardized testing of all homeschooling children.

You might guess that states with more regulation produced better-prepared kids. Interestingly enough, it has been shown that test scores are actually higher in the less-regulated states. My theory is that less regulation gives parents more time to actually teach their children!

Colleges vary regarding the requirements for admission of homeschoolers. Some require kids to have a GED. Others require the COMPASS test, which is a math and English placement exam. Others ask that parents fill out a detailed transcript, describing the course work that the student completed in high school. But homeschooled students are welcomed—even recruited—at every university in the United States. Colleges have found that homeschooled students typically are well prepared, highly motivated, and possess excellent study skills.

What Is It Really Like?

People wonder what a typical homeschooling day in a large family looks like. Every family is different, but here is what school looks like at our house. We usually get breakfast cleanup and Bible study done by 9:30 a.m. or so. Typically, my teenagers need four or five hours to complete their school for the day, and my elementary-aged kids get done with all their subjects in two and a half or three hours. My teenagers work independently, usually in their bedrooms, coming to me only when they get stuck or have a question about an assignment. Elementary-age kids need more direction than older kids, so they work near me at the dining room table.

With the number of children that I have, I don't expect to get anything except school done in the mornings. Once I've helped the elementary kids through their math and handwriting, I get reading and phonics done with kids one by one. This year I am not doing science with my elementary-age kids; instead, we're focusing on writing skills. Next year, when our two new girls' English language skills are a little stronger, I will run all the grade schoolers through an excellent science text.

Lots of people think science must be taught every year. A few years ago, I met Dr. Jay Wile, the author of the Apologia Science curriculum. He told me that most elementary science curriculums cover the same topics repetitively from year to year, adding just a little more detail each year. Intelligent kids don't need six years to learn this information. A thorough immersion in a good science curriculum during the last couple years of elementary school will teach a child everything he needs to know.

We break for lunch around 1:00 p.m. If the day has gone well, the majority of the school that involves me is done. Often, I'll need to read with a child or two after lunch. Kids usually do their thirty minutes of independent reading after lunch as well. Teenagers work into mid-afternoon before their studies are concluded. In the afternoons, we straighten the house, play outside, and run errands.

Helping Children Work

Whether you're homeschooling or just helping a couple of kids with math worksheets in the evenings, I'm sure you're familiar with this dilemma: as soon as you settle in to help one child with a math problem, another child will be suddenly frantic to get your attention, directing volleys of "Mom! Mom! Mom!" your way until you're ready to scream.

This school year I have five kids in elementary school. This makes for some crazy study times. I learned to stagger the subjects so that no more than two kids were doing math at any one time, since math requires lots of mom help. But for awhile I was still frustrated when multiple kids would need help at once. I hated being interrupted when I was trying to help one child, and I also hated that nothing was getting done while they frantically waved their hands and/or twiddled their pencils as they impatiently waited for my attention.

I decided first of all to make sure that each child always had at least three possible subjects lined up in front of him. Alongside the open math book, I'd set the handwriting book and the reading book. I told my kids that if they were stuck on math, they were *not* to interrupt or sit waving their hand frantically. Instead, they should do the following:

1. Skim the math lesson for other problems they can do unassisted.
2. Do their handwriting assignment for the day.
3. Get a jump-start on their required half-hour of independent reading each day.

Then I made flags. Each flag is just a little paper rectangle taped to a wooden skewer. Because I wanted the flags to be freestanding (leaving the kids' hands free to keep working!) I stuck the point end of each skewer into a tub of play dough, right through the lid of the tub. This let the flags stand up nicely. I made four, labeled one through four.

During school time, I keep the flags in the center of the table, where four of my kids work. If a kid gets stuck on an assignment while I am occupied, he takes the number-one flag. The second kid gets number two, and so forth. That way, when I look up from helping one kid, I can tell who is next.

It may sound a little impersonal to tell your kid to take a number, but my kids really like the system because they know whose turn is next. Once they've grabbed their flag, they can go back to working on another math problem or begin another assignment. This helps them work more efficiently and encourages them to think about a problem just a little longer. Sometimes they even have the problem solved by the time I get there.

This has made our mornings much quieter and less distracting. Although I came up with this idea for use during homeschooling, I bet it would be just as useful for a parent trying to get two or three kids through evening homework time. One mom even told me she was going to try giving her only child a flag, to avoid being constantly interrupted in her own work in the evenings.

Hints for Teaching When You Have Preschoolers

I've found my morning goes best if I spend a few minutes with my two youngest children first. We read a story and then I usually try to lay out at least a couple of play areas for the younger children. I got the idea from a book on Montessori education for preschoolers. I used it a lot when I had twin preschoolers who got into everything, and I do it in a more casual way for my three- and five-year-old daughters now.

Play stations are just self-contained activities that children can do on their own in various corners of the room. Usually, I'll have two or three activities set up at the start of the school day, near where I'll be working with my older children.

Good play-area activities include Legos, Fisher-Price houses, water paints, pop beads, lacing cards, crayons and paper, and books on tape. Some activities can be easily shared; other activities are best done one at a time. I encourage children to stick with activities for at least ten or fifteen minutes before moving on to the next thing. Sometimes I'll set the timer; other times I'll let them move around in a more casual way, giving kids more time with activities that seem more interesting that morning.

Younger children will have shorter attention spans, but the idea is to encourage children to stick with each activity for a little while instead of flitting from place to place. At first, children may resist or say an activity is boring. When my kids do that, I tell them that they can either do the activity or lie down and take a rest on the couch. If you kindly but firmly enforce the rules, they usually decide playing is more fun than lying down. Doing this on a regular basis will help children increase their attention spans.

One activity that was a huge hit at my house recently involved setting my preschoolers on a sturdy bench at the sink. I put a couple of big pots in the sink, which they were allowed to fill with water. I gave them mixing spoons and some shaker containers of old spices that I hadn't used in awhile. Their job was to make "spice soup." The two of them worked happily for over an hour. This activity was so engrossing that I will definitely remember it for the future. If you don't happen to have any old spices, get some at the dollar store or buy them in bulk at your local grocery store.

Another fun winter activity is to set a roasting pan full of uncooked rice in the middle of a bedsheet on the kitchen floor. Give your child scoops and ladles and measuring cups and maybe even a child's dish set. He'll have a great time playing just like in the sandbox. When you're done, you can use the bedsheet to funnel the rice back into the pan, then set it aside for play another day.

One final note: my house is always a mess by lunchtime. I ignore it as much as I can during school. Every day after lunch we work together to clean up the house. Even the preschoolers help with the work. If a little one resists cleaning up, I'll send her to bed until she is strong enough to obey. Usually five minutes of boredom in the bedroom is enough to get the child back out and helping.

Sometimes, if a child is really resistant, I will physically guide her hands in picking up a few things, then say, "Are you strong enough to do it on your own, or do you need more help?" Almost all self-respecting little kids will decide they'd much rather control their own hands than have mom guide them, even if it does mean obeying!

People often think that homeschooling takes a tremendous amount of organization and work. Of course there's work. But there are also great advantages. I love the additional time I have with my kids. I love watching that light bulb go on as they learn new concepts. And I really love the relaxed, rush-free time we have together in the mornings before school starts.

What If My Children Don't Learn Something That They Need to Know?

It can be intimidating to feel like your children's future success is solely your responsibility. Some people end up deciding to homeschool to take more control over their children's education. Others decide to leave school to the "experts" in the public education system. Still others opt for private schools that specialize in classical education or the arts or faith-based schooling. No matter the choices we make for our children, we all sometimes wonder if our children will miss out on something because of the choices we've made. What if there are gaps in our children's education?

Here's something that a lot of people don't realize. All kids come out of school with "gaps," no matter what type of schooling they've had. Didn't you? Chances are, you have had to look up a few things since you graduated from school, and most likely you've gotten along just fine.

But if we can instill in our children an ethic of hard work, the ability to read, and a curiosity about the world, they will have the tools they need to overcome any gaps they may have.

ENCOURAGING SIBLING FRIENDSHIPS

Why Can't They Be Friends?

An indelible memory of my childhood is of being left to babysit my younger siblings. I must have been twelve or so. I remember my parents sauntering off, hand in hand, to vote at the public school right behind our house. They couldn't have been gone more than half an hour, but I used the time to the hilt. I climbed up on the kitchen counter, got into the spice cupboard, and coaxed my adoring younger siblings to taste-test various delicacies—ginger, black pepper, curry powder.

Oh, the red faces! The coughing! The sputtering! It was the best fun I'd had in weeks. I even coaxed some of them to come back for seconds. I still don't know why my folks trusted me—or why my siblings forgave me. But somehow they did. And now we laugh about it.

Parents dream of siblings becoming lifelong friends. Siblings can be a source of support and acceptance and shared memory that is hard to duplicate in the broader world. Though outside friendships are also wonderful, adults who are close to their siblings in adulthood tend to value those relationships over all others.

Colleen is the fifth of nine children and talks about the joy that those relationships bring to her life:

When you live in a large family, you're bound to have at least a sibling or two that you become best friends with. Maybe it's that sibling that is close to you in age, where you really pushed each other's buttons until you learned where they all were. Or maybe you are the eldest and you really connected well with the baby of the family to the point where you feel a certain sense of protectiveness that you don't have for other siblings. It's not that you don't love all your siblings, but you may not exactly click with all their spouses or the way they parent. There is that one (or, hopefully, more) who you would trust your kids to if you died suddenly, the one who maybe married someone whose personality is similar to your spouse's and you can just pick up the phone and chat for hours with them.

Sometimes, while pulling young combatants apart, it can be hard for a parent to see far enough into the future to imagine siblings living peacefully in the same hemisphere, let alone spending hours on the phone chatting. But even in the thick of childhood squabbling, there are real benefits to having a bunch of siblings. Alicia, oldest of seven, shares her experience:

My sisters and I share a unique history, memories of the same home, and struggles with and deep love for the same parents. Three of my brothers are still teenagers, and I love getting to know them as they mature into men and not just as the sweet babies I tended to. I am so grateful for my family.

The Influence of Siblings on Self-Esteem

We often think that it is mostly younger kids who benefit from older siblings. Older kids teach younger ones how to wear their hair and throw knuckleballs and make the splashiest cannonballs. Younger ones watch older ones do everything first, and because of that, they learn more about the way things are done before they ever have to do things themselves. Most often, younger kids are portrayed as no better than irritations in the lives of older children. But that is a very incomplete picture.

There are true benefits to growing up as an older sibling, and they extend beyond gaining a reputation as an experienced babysitter. Older kids can learn much about patience from little ones. They see firsthand the need to make accommodations for weaker, smaller people. They become accustomed to reaching out to give a hand to someone in need. A few years of living with preschoolers can mean that when kids become parents themselves, they'll be less surprised at the inevitable toddler tantrums and lost shoes. And never underestimate the power of hero worship on a teenager's developing psyche. Megan, the oldest of six, discovered how her little brother could brighten her day:

> *I found that when I was a teenager, the only thing that could shake off my angst from the day was a rousing wrestle session with my two-year-old brother. He was by far the most adorable child and such a riot. I'm sure my Mom accomplished a lot while I was keeping him occupied! I actually felt sorry for my friends who did not have such a household that seemed "fully alive."*

Our three-year-old loves her thirteen-year-old brother, Daniel. Instead of using his name, she calls him "my boy!" Only Daniel gets that designation. Her tone is rich with warm pride. It brings a smile to every face in the family, even the ones not fortunate enough to be called "my boy!"

Relationships like that foster self-esteem in a rich and wonderful way. The unconditional love that a toddler can rain down on an older

Sometimes, while pulling young combatants apart,
it can be hard for a parent to see far enough into
the future to imagine siblings living peacefully
in the same hemisphere . . .

sibling can be pure balm, especially on days when mom and dad are being difficult, and there's not much that's more fun than whispering late at night with the brother or sister who shares your room.

Helping Kids Enjoy Their Time Together

Making the most of harmonious moments is a big part of encouraging siblings to be friends. Cathy, a mother of three, says that she tries to say yes whenever an activity will promote friendship:

My kids love having sleepovers in each other's rooms. It's easy to say no when I'm right in the middle of cooking dinner or doing laundry or on the phone. [Especially] if it's going to take some effort on my part, it's hard to say yes to my kids. But those are the VERY times I need to say yes because it's usually something they want to do together. It's a pain for me, because I'm the one that has to drag out the blankets and sheets and sleeping bags, and it takes them FOREVER to fall asleep. But when I hear them giggling in their rooms and talking about fun things they want to do together this summer, it's priceless. Or they might ask to have a water fight or to dig a huge hole in our yard or to have a lemonade stand or to make a dinosaur out of papier-mâché, etc. Whatever it is, it usually requires some work on my part (read: huge clean up!!!), but it's a small price to pay if it gets my kids working together, building memories, and playing well.

I also try to support my children when they are playing well together. Too often the vibes don't flow so well, so it makes sense to keep the fun rolling as long as possible. Sometimes I'll delay dinner or do one of their chores myself, or on a lovely summer evening I'll even put off bedtime for awhile.

Homeschooling and Sibling Relationships

Sometimes people will ask if I am worried about my kids getting enough socialization since they are homeschooled. I always laugh. "Are you kidding? With nine brothers and sisters, the real challenge is finding a few minutes alone."

And when you think about it, relationships with friends are a breeze compared to sibling relationships. If my kids can learn to get along with their siblings, chances are they'll have no trouble navigating less complicated relationships with friends.

One of my favorite lines from the movie *Treasure Planet* is when Delbert says, "Familiarity breeds . . . well . . . umm . . . contempt." Unfortunately, kids all have moments of contempt for their siblings. You would think that when they reach school age, their relationship with their siblings might benefit from having a break from each other during the school day. We discovered the opposite to be true.

When our oldest was five years old, we sent her off to a local Christian school, where she attended kindergarten and first grade. Within a few weeks, I noticed a subtle change in the way that she related to her younger siblings. Before, she played happily with them, but now that she was a big-school kid, she seemed to feel that she was too old for them. Instead, she constantly begged to have her new school friends over for sleepovers and play dates.

I was delighted that she was making new friends, but I was grieved that these new friendships seemed to be coming at the expense of her relationship with her siblings. When she reached second grade, we decided, for a variety of other reasons, to begin homeschooling. One of the happiest side effects of that difficult choice was the rebirth of her friendship with her younger sister and brothers. We were all glad to have her back.

Encouraging Kindness

Often, kids need help navigating the sea of sibling relationships. Most parents experience frustration over the way that their children fight. It doesn't matter if there are three kids or ten; getting along is tough.

Especially painful to parents is the way kids zero in on each other's weaknesses. If a kid doesn't like his glasses, his sibling will mention them every chance he gets. They'll diss each other's music choices or laugh when they make mistakes. It can be so saddening to see kids pushing each other's buttons over and over.

When I notice my kids picking on other children's weaknesses, I pick a quiet time to speak directly to the person who is being unkind. "Have you noticed how Ben really hates to wear his glasses?" Usually, the child will admit that he has. If he pretends ignorance of the issue, I'll explain the other child's feelings in a non-accusatory way and ask the child if he will help me support his brother. "Could you help me make sure nobody teases him about his glasses? Let me know if anyone does, okay?"

Enlisting the child's help as his brother's protector will often discourage teasing.

Enlisting the child's help as his brother's protector will often discourage teasing. You may not even have to mention the child's part in the teasing. Most likely his conscience will do that work. If we can teach our children to make allowance for the weaknesses of others, we will be encouraging a kinder gentler spirit in our home.

Eggshells

It also helps to get creative when you're trying to make a point with a child who is upset. Recently, one of my older girls was very upset with her nine-year-old brother. The slight was small in reality but felt huge to her. She simmered around in a hostile way for a day or so, refusing to talk or even make eye contact with him. He is a sensitive child and felt her anger very deeply, but he didn't know what to do beyond the apology that he had already given and that she had ignored.

He opted to steer clear of her to avoid her simmering hostility. She then interpreted his avoidance of her as more evidence that he didn't like her. She was so full of irritation that she couldn't see that it wasn't hate he was feeling—it was sadness.

I addressed the issue directly at first, reminding her that he'd said sorry and she needed to forgive him. She was too angry to hear me, insisting that he was the one at fault. I knew how deeply he was hurt by her unforgiveness, but I didn't know how to make her see how much she was hurting him.

After several minutes of unfruitful talk, she stormed off, certain of the rightness of her cause. I thought for a minute. Then I went and found a rock and an egg and a bowl. I went to her and sat down in front of her. She was sitting on the floor in the hall with her head in her arms. Without saying a word, I cracked the egg into a little bowl.

At the sound of the egg cracking and plopping into the bowl, she looked up in surprise.

"See this rock?" I said, holding up the rock. "See how hard it is? You think your brother is like this rock, but he isn't." I then crunched a bit of the eggshell from the broken egg between my fingers. "Your brother's heart is like this eggshell. It's not strong. It breaks easily. He is really sad because you're angry at him."

She quickly went into a rant about how mean he was and how much he hated her. I let her talk awhile, but then I cradled the broken egg in my hand and covered it with my other hand. "Maybe he's acting brave, trying to cover up his sadness with loud talk." I took my hand away to reveal the shattered eggshell. "But inside, his heart is like this broken egg. He feels really sad that you are mad at him."

I could see her face soften as she looked at the ruins of the egg. I reminded her that Jesus asks us to forgive, even when people hurt us, even when it is not easy. I didn't get a promise to forgive at that very moment, but I could tell I'd given her something to think about. Later, when I spotted her playing happily with her brother, I breathed a sigh of relief.

Back Off

Some kids have a hard time admitting their own part in a disagreement. With a child like that, it is often more productive to ask the child to forgive than to say sorry. Saying sorry is an extremely difficult thing to do in the heat of anger. But if you can coax a child to forgive, their hearts often soften enough to face up to their own part in the argument and then be sorry for what they have done.

Another tactic that has helped to diffuse anger at our house lately is one we saw when we were watching reruns of *The Cosby Show*. In one episode, Heathcliff was coaching his daughter's boyfriend how to respond when she started to fly off the handle and get irritated over little things.

He said that the best thing to do was to back off—spread your arms apart and literally step back from the argument before it escalated. We all laughed at his mannerisms as he explained this tactic to the young man. But a day later I realized that was a perfect response for anyone when they're realizing a loved one is starting to lose it.

Disengage. Step back. Since then I have reminded kids several times of that option—complete with a comic overexaggeration of that step back—and kids have been very responsive. I am not always able to come up with such a creative way to make a point with a child. But when I think creatively and playfully, I find that my words are much more effective. I truly believe that if we can teach kids to be kind and forgiving to their siblings, they have the tools they need to get along with almost anyone.

Teaching Kids to Take Responsibility in Relationships

Not long ago, I left the teenagers in charge while I went out to run errands for a few hours. When I came back, I knew it hadn't gone well. The seventeen- and fifteen-year-olds fled to their rooms the instant I walked into the house, and the emotions of the younger set ranged from pouting to anxious defensiveness to outright crying. When I inquired about the morning's happening, some of the children skirted around my questions. Others hurried to share stories in aggrieved tones of voice. None of the stories seemed to match.

I knew from experience that in a situation like this it is hard to sort out who is to blame. It takes two to fight. Rarely is one person utterly blameless. And frankly, after listening to two kids whine simultaneously for only a minute, I was already too tired to figure it out. I could tell no one had been mortally wounded, but I could also tell there were a lot of people who were sure the blame lay with someone else. I decided to try something different.

I gathered everyone together in the family room and told them that I could tell the morning hadn't gone very well. Again, I was barraged with attempts to implicate other siblings. I called a time-out right then and there.

"Nope. This time I'm not going to listen to you complain about each other. Here's what we're going to do: I want every person in this room to list *one* thing that you yourself could have done to help the morning go better."

There were sulky faces around the room. No one wanted to take any blame, and, frankly, I wasn't even sure if the younger kids would understand what I was asking. But then, into the silence, the five-year-old spoke up: "I could decide to not hit Erika."

"Right!" I said. "Good idea." I turned to the next-youngest kid. "You're next. What could you have done differently?"

Sheepishly, he answered me. "Not tease Lidya."

Joshua admitted that he should have emptied the dishwasher when Jared told him to, and so we went around the room. A couple of kids had a hard time admitting they may have done wrong. After hearing the admissions of several other kids, I had a better idea of what had happened, and so was able to gently suggest that one sister should have used kinder words. "Yeah," she admitted grudgingly.

Though I had needed to feed her the words to name her error, even that mollified her aggrieved sibling. It was amazing to see the subtle shift of mood in the room as each child accepted responsibility, however small, for a part in the fighting. Faces softened. Hostility trickled away. Not only did this allow kids to think more about their own role in the disagreement but it also made it easier for the injured parties to forgive—this even though I did not ask the kids to directly apologize to each other.

I have used this tactic several times since then, and it has worked well each time. I think that these days there is a tremendous emphasis on self-protection, on making sure no one wrongs you. But I don't want my kids to grow up hostile and defensive. Instead, I hope to help my children be forgiving and to focus on what they can do to improve a situation. No matter how bad the situation may be, usually you can do something to make it better.

Christy, a mother of four, does a similar debriefing with her children when she finds them fighting:

> *I have held my boys, now ten and thirteen, responsible to varying degrees when others began the altercation. My big question to them is: "When was the very first moment you*

*knew there was trouble?" That is the moment you remove
yourself from the situation, not after you've been cornered or
challenged. They have been quite able to rewind back to that
moment and rewrite how the action should have played out.*

Easing the Adjustment to New Siblings

A challenging time for many families is when a new child comes into
the family. A few years back, Melissa Fay Greene, author of *There is No
Me Without You*, wrote an interesting article about mega-families called
"The Family Mobile." In it she compared a growing family to a mobile.

> *"I imagine a homely contraption of wire hangers and dangling
> threads with plastic dolls swinging at their ends. In times of
> tranquility, the mobile is balanced. When a new child arrives . . .
> the family is thrown into disequilibrium [like a] wind chime in
> the gales of a storm."*

This is a great picture to keep in mind after adding a new family
member. Certainly, adopting a couple of older children, like my husband
and I did in 2007, will throw the balance of a family off for awhile. But
even an infant changes the order of things. Suddenly, the two-year-old
has to wait while the baby nurses. You find yourself less tolerant of the
six-year-old's tantrums—shouldn't she have outgrown them by now?
And your husband's needs for conversation with his wife are trumped by
your need to sleep.

The first thing we can do to help our children accept new family
members is to share our own excitement over the new arrivals. When
we were waiting for our sixth child to come home, our fifth child wasn't
even two years old. But he prayed every evening for his new brother.

If our kids see our excitement over the new arrivals, they will pick
up on it, and often their excitement will mirror our own. But we need

The first thing we can do to help our children accept new family members is to share our own excitement over the new arrivals.

to reassure them it is okay to have some negative feelings too. Talk about the way that baby is going to need a lot of mom's attention, and sometimes that will mean that the older children have to wait to talk with mom.

It also helps to have some plans in place and to talk about those plans with your children. Maybe you can have a treat basket in the pantry so that preschoolers can run and get their own snack while the baby is nursing. Maybe you can set a heap of books out or have a special craft for the moments when mom is busy. Occasional play dates with grandma or a beloved aunt can also help a child see how important he or she still is.

Jane, a mother of six, shares how she helped her children prepare for the adoption of two siblings from Ethiopia:

> *We talked frequently both as a whole family and in smaller one-on-one conversations about our new kids. We prayed for them nightly, at first in a general sense, but later—once we knew them—we prayed for them by name. Our children all accompanied us to the store to select items for the welcome bags—everyone was able to include something. They helped select and/or take photos for the family albums. We prepared bedrooms and selected photo frames to begin displaying our new-kid pictures around the house in prominent locations.*
>
> *At the suggestion of a friend, we added our two new children to our family operations center prior to their arrival*

and even selected job cards for them each Sunday. The
resident kids pitched in to help do the new-kid jobs until their
homecoming, which was a real motivator for our two older
children to anticipate the swift arrival of their chore helpers!

Our oldest son (twelve) accompanied my husband to
Ethiopia to bring our kids home. Our three girls (eight, three,
and two) helped ready the house and make giant welcome-
home signs to bring to the airport for their arrival. Did it make
a difference? I can't say for sure as this is the only time we've
adopted. But what I can say for certain, however, is that by
the time H and Baby T walked through the customs gate, our
children ran those final few steps into each other's arms in
what might have seemed to the unknowing onlooker a long-
awaited reunion.

What to Do When the Family Mood Goes Sour

Every family has times when the family mood is not as cheery as it could
be, when people seem to be snipping and sniping at each other in an
unusually persistent way. What can you do to boost your family morale?

First, think about the happiest times you have spent together. Maybe
it was when you were on vacation. Obviously, you can't vacation all the
time. But maybe you could fit in some of the fun things that you did do
while on vacation. Maybe you can go on a bike ride together or visit the
children's museum.

Our family sets aside Friday evenings as movie night. We pop some
popcorn, line up the bean-bag chairs to provide front-row seating for
the younger kids, and settle in to enjoy our time together.

Once, we all wrote notes about each other. Everyone in the family
listed something they liked about every other family member. The
younger kids dictated their lists to me, and the older ones wrote their

own. I compiled all the positive things about each person onto one sheet of paper and presented each person with this list of good things about him or herself. This was a great morale boost for each person. It was meaningful to hear good words from every other family member. Years later, most of us have saved our letters. Even John and I find them to be very significant.

Another thing that we do sometimes is to assign secret pals. People are to do three kind things each day for their secret pal. At the end of the day, we each try to guess who our secret pal was. It is perfectly fine to do kind things for other family members as well, to make it harder for people to guess who their secret pal is.

How about a Game Night?

One of our favorite morale boosters is family game night. We've discovered a bunch of games that are fun for large numbers of people. Some games are totally chance and can easily be played by people of all different ages. If there is an element of skill involved, you can often weight the game so that even the less-skilled younger players have a chance at winning. You can do this by giving an older person more cards or more chips that he or she must get rid of before winning. Or you can allow a younger player a little more latitude with the way he lays down his cards.

In UNO, you lay cards down in sequence, matching either the color or the number of the card laid down before it. There are also draw cards and wild cards that allow you to change the color of card being currently played. When we play UNO with toddlers, we just let them lay down whichever card they want, whether it matches or not. We play on whatever they put down. Basically, a two-year-old is just another "wild" card. Soon enough, they learn their colors and are able to play by the real rules.

Apples to Apples is a funny fast-moving game and can be played by many people of any age. Though it is a language-based game, it doesn't matter in the least if the little kids can't read the cards they lay down. Often, the cards they select by chance are just as funny/applicable as the ones carefully chosen by people who can actually read.

Scum is another fun game for a group of at least four people and can be played by anyone who recognizes their numbers. It is best to play this game at a table. During the course of the game, there is a lot of movement around the table, with some people assigned to be king, queen, scum, and assistant scum. You can find complete game instructions at http://scribbit.blogspot.com/2007/05/president-and-scum.html.

Dominoes is a fairly simple game, though preschoolers will probably need a bit of help counting their dots and arranging their dominoes in sequence. When we play this game with several young ones, we just assign the youngest ones a handler to give them advice and to help them during the game. If you have two sets of dominoes, you may be able to coax toddlers to simply play with the second set while sitting alongside the real players.

Dutch Blitz is an extremely fast-moving game for up to four people. You can get the cards at www.amazon.com. This game is almost identical to Nertz, a game which you can play with four different decks of cards. You can find the rules for Nertz at http://www.answers.com/nertz?cat=entertainment.

Phase Ten is a card game we enjoy at our house. It can be played with lots of people. It is a little more complex, and most kids need to be six or seven to play without help. But it is my favorite way to play with my kids on a quiet afternoon.

Creative Consequences

Sometimes consequences are necessary to discourage repeated unkindness between kids. One of the most effective consequences I have found is to have the offender do a job for the child whom he hurt. A kid can make his sister's bed or fold his brother's laundry or do his Saturday housecleaning chores. Often, when kids are not getting along, the last thing they want to do is help each other out. Being assigned to help each other is a strong disincentive to fighting.

Sometimes "weaker" kids can be masters at goading aggressive siblings into actions that then get the aggressor in trouble. When I suspect a case like that, I will sometimes have both children do a job for the other child. But really the tactic is most effective when you can sort out the person most at fault and have him or her make up for his action with work.

Don't be too discouraged if it seems to take years for sibling relationships to grow. They tend to improve greatly as children mature. Our eldest came back from her first year of college with a whole new appreciation for her younger brothers.

The Importance of Keeping Kids' Emotional Tanks Full

I've come to realize that fighting between children is most intense when they are having a hard time getting their own needs met. If a kid is feeling neglected or out of sorts, he can't have the emotional energy to speak gently to another child, to forgive, to be kind. Often I can trace an increase of fighting in the family directly to a too-busy schedule, especially a too-busy momma, or to a too-great focus on accomplishment at the expense of family fun.

It is an exhausting job as a parent to realize that so much is up to us, to keep putting in, to keep giving, to keep filling those emotional tanks. But that is exactly what we need to do. We parents are responsible for the emotional climate of the home.

Kids need compliments for small accomplishments. They need parents to see their little flashes of brilliance. They need us to laugh at the jokes and admire their cartwheel attempts. Of course, they need lots of hugs—though in the case of teenaged boys, a friendly punch in the arm or an offer to arm wrestle may be more effective.

I find that on days when I consciously make an effort to touch my children more—to give hugs and back scratches and pats on the shoulder—those days seem to go better and be less filled with fighting. Touch is a very powerful tool.

As important as your contribution as a parent is, don't be too hard on yourself if your best efforts don't seem to make a difference. Kids also are responsible for their own moods and actions. I am comforted to remember that God is my children's parent too and that he can speak to their hearts in a way that I cannot. And he can mend relationships as well.

Vera, a mother of five, also takes comfort in knowing that God is working too:

> *My favorite thing to remind myself of when I hear kids fighting is that God is working things into and out of them now, at very young ages, that are very hard to have worked on when you are older. These kids will never struggle with not knowing how to deal with other people. They are learning now to understand and accept people's differences. They are learning how to communicate their own desires and how to deal with it when those desires are not met. How many adults are learning those same lessons but with many years of behavior already ingrained in them?*

In the 2005 remake of the movie *Yours, Mine and Ours,* the kids in the newly blended family spend much of the movie fighting with each other. But there's a scene near the end of the movie that I love. One of the children is getting picked on by kids at school. The other kids rally around the bullies, forming a wall of protection around their siblings, and the bullies run off in fear.

This is a Hollywood dramatization of the power in a big clan. But talk to people who grew up in big families, and over and over again they will talk about the closeness and camaraderie. I know that I didn't truly appreciate my family until I was grown, and I suspect that may be the case for lots of kids. But if we as parents can help our children experience that kind of camaraderie, they may not have to wait till adulthood.

The Power of Teamwork

Awhile back, I was sighing over the state of our raspberry bed. It is about thirty feet long and three feet deep, and when the kids heard me talking, I could just see them bracing themselves for the inevitable work. Instead of assigning the job to just one or two kids, as I've been known to do, I told everyone we were going to work all together, and we were only going to work for forty-five minutes.

The teenagers and I worked deep in the raspberry bed. The middle kids weeded a section that had been weeded a few weeks before and wasn't quite so bad. The five- and three-year-olds found their little red wagon, filled it with weeds, and dragged it to the burn pile. It only took two trips to wear them out. But by then, my middle-sized kids had gotten tired of weeding and were glad to take over the weed hauling.

If I had only assigned a couple of kids to the job, they would have made very little impact on the space in forty-five minutes. But by bringing everyone together and working alongside them myself—a huge key!—we were able to do so much more.

Afterwards, as we sat on the deck sucking on Popsicles, I made sure to praise my kids to high heaven so they would recognize that power. "Look how much we got accomplished by working together!"

It can take a lot of work to help children become friends. But the payoff—strong friendships that your children will carry with them for life—is more than worth all that work.

CELEBRATING EACH CHILD

Will They Know How Special They Are to Me?

This chapter speaks to one of my greatest longings as a parent. I want each of my children to know how very special he or she is to me. Sometimes in the middle of parenting, it can feel easier to make one decision for multiple children. But making a conscious effort to treat each child as an individual is at the heart of helping a child feel loved.

As a music lover, I always assumed all our children would take piano lessons. I started piano lessons for our oldest four children en masse when they ranged in ages from five to eleven. Enthusiasm ran high—for the first month. Then the complaining began.

"I already practiced!" (Chopsticks? For two minutes?)

"Why do I have to practice again?" (Because your piano lesson is in two hours and you've practiced half an hour all week!)

We struggled through lessons for a year or so. I hoped if we persevered long enough, eventually, they would grow to love it. But at $12 per lesson per child per week, it was getting expensive. And it was miserable. Three out of the four children hated the lessons and begged to quit nearly every week. They only practiced when I nagged, and because they weren't really interested, it took weeks to learn a single song.

But the one child who loved it—our daughter Erika—really, really loved it. She practiced an hour or two a day for the sheer joy of it. She requested new piano books for her birthday and Christmas, and because her interest in it was her own, she progressed at an amazing rate.

Seeing the difference between her and the other children opened our eyes. We were dealing with unique individuals here. Forcing them all to learn piano was not honoring that uniqueness. When I reluctantly gave up my little fantasy of childish musical perfection, everyone breathed a huge sigh of relief—including the piano lover, who was delighted to call piano her personal domain.

I've spoken with moms who make the opposite decision for their families. They feel that the short-term discomfort of coaxing a child to do something he doesn't love is an acceptable price to pay for a child who grows up to be a musician. They treat music lessons just like multiplication tables—a requirement whether the child is interested or not.

I see the logic behind that choice. I admire the gumption and resolve it takes to keep a child applied to something they do not love. But that choice was not the right one for my family.

Our piano lover is now an excellent pianist. She plays for church and for pleasure. Music is a true joy to her. Of my children who hated piano lessons, two of them sing in the church choir, and all three love to listen to music. They're not all musicians. But they're all music lovers. That's good enough for me.

Cookie-Cutter Parenting

Cookie cutter parenting is so tempting. It's easier to make each choice once and then not have to rethink it. Buying someone a new shirt? You might as well get one for everyone so no one will feel left out. Already spend half your life at the baseball field? It wouldn't make that much difference to sign up the little kids too. Buying one kid a kazoo? Why not buy half a dozen? (I promise, you'll only do that once!)

Part of this mentality is sheer practicality. Similar-age kids often enjoy similar things, and it is easier to buy in bulk than to be constantly breaking up fights over new items. We want to give kids equal opportunities. But sometimes equal is not the same thing as fair. Think about it: you can't make life fair for kids anyway, no matter how hard you try.

In our own family, we have one child on whom we spend thousands more dollars every year. Unfair? Maybe. But he was born with only one foot and needs his $12,000 prosthetic leg rebuilt every year. Going through life with one foot isn't fair either, but it is reality for some people.

We all have unique life experiences and needs. When we parent our children as if we can somehow make things come out even—cutting cake with a ruler or buying every child in the family a pair of shoes just because you bought a pair for one—we're actually training our children to squabble more. We're training them to be hyper-vigilant to every perceived injustice. It is far better to teach our children that, no, life isn't fair but we as parents will do our best to make sure that our children's needs are met. Sometimes, that means buying an ice cream cone for everyone. Other times, we buy shoes for the kid who lost his in the lake, while the more responsible family members get to wear their old ones. Still, other times, that means sitting in the bedroom with a child having a bad day and letting him cry in your arms while the other kids sit out in the living room and watch *Cars* for the tenth time.

Sometimes, when a child is all bent out of shape over another kid who gets an extra bite of cake or a fun outing, I'll remind the child that it goes both ways. "Remember when your sister stepped on a nail and got a tetanus shot? I didn't make you get a tetanus shot too, did I? Different people need different things, but I'll do my best to make sure you get everything you really need."

Of course, I don't condone showing massive favoritism to one child. That can be terribly hurtful. But we do our kids a favor by teaching them to tolerate and even expect inequality at times.

As a Christian, I believe that God will meet our needs in just the right way, no matter how it feels at the time, and I share that belief with my children. As kids get older, you can talk with them about the opportunities they have by virtue of where they were born or who their family is. Many children in this world will never drink clean water or walk through the door of a school. Part of being a happy and responsible human is being more aware of our blessings than of our lacks.

Especially in a large family, trying to make things exactly even can get terribly expensive. (Case in point: those $200-per-month piano lessons that only one child enjoyed.) It is much better to discover what interests each child and nurture those interests. Recognizing instead of minimizing that uniqueness in each child nurtures their souls.

I strongly believe that part of what makes living in a large family good for a child is his parents' ability to see him as unique. It's true for adults too. Would you rather work for a boss who has twenty people doing the exact same task or would you rather have a niche where you are the expert?

Children all need opportunities, but they don't need the exact same opportunities. Our children are unique. Our parenting of them should honor that uniqueness rather than trying to cram them into one mold that doesn't quite fit anyone.

Know Your Child

It can be hard work figuring out exactly what makes our kids tick, what brings them joy. But the dividends can be enormous. One essential key is not to allow children to fill all their hours of downtime with TV and video games.

Multitudes of boys dream of becoming video game designers. While there is nothing inherently wrong with that choice, the sheer numbers of kids interested in this career mean the competition is going to be fierce. I think that so many boys call this their future career simply because it is their only leisure experience in life.

They've never had the fun of building a scrap-wood clubhouse on the back lot, or getting good at drawing, or plowing through some really good literature. Even the video-game junkies often have never ripped into their own computer to perform an upgrade. At our house, we try to limit video-game time to an hour a day. My bigger boys, who are learning computer languages, can spend an additional hour a day working on Web pages or fiddling with HTML or JavaScript. But limiting the computer allows kids time to think.

Never underestimate the power of downtime—even outright boredom. If we fill every minute with activities, kids don't have time to think creatively, to read, and to discover what intrigues and excites them. Reading is a crucial interest that can be so easily squeezed out by too much TV or gaming. One of the most precious gifts we can give our kids is the chance to find their own niche in the world. Kids who know they are good at something are much less susceptible to peer pressure and depression.

Our younger children are still discovering their niches. But of the older ones, we have one interested in literature and history, another who loves piano and math, another whose love is computer science, and a fourth who is a budding cartoonist.

The following sections share some specific guidance for learning more about your child's personality type. You may find it helpful to write each of your children's names down the side of a piece of paper before you read this section and jot notes about each child as you read through each section.

Love Languages

To be happy in their family, children need to feel your love. The problem is, different actions are most effective for different kids. You will touch your children's souls most deeply if you learn to speak in their own language. A book that illuminates the various personality types is *The Five Love Languages* by Gary Chapman.

It is especially important for mothers of large families to take time to figure out what motivates their kids. By using the love language that speaks most directly to each child's heart, we maximize the impact of the time that we have to invest interacting with our children. Of course, kids need both quantity time and quality time. But we can more effectively get to the heart of their concerns by speaking their own language. Visit http://www.fivelovelanguages.com/forfamilies.html for more information.

As you read through these descriptions, keep in mind that your child may be a mix of several languages. But he probably has one language that reassures him most. Ask yourself the following questions as you read the descriptions below:

- How does your child express love to the people around him? People most naturally express love to others in their own dominant love language.
- What does your child request most often? Children often request what they need the most.
- What does your child complain about most often? He may be sharing a need for more of his preferred love style.

Words of Affirmation

We all appreciate praise. But the child whose love language is words of affirmation feels most encouraged when we verbalize the positives we have noticed and when we encourage with words during tough times. Mark Twain once said, "I can live for two months on a good compliment." This is definitely true of a person whose primary love language is words of affirmation.

If you grew up in a home where praise was scarce, you may have a hard time affirming your child with words. Some people fear that if they praise too much, their kids will get a swelled head or quit working, especially if the child is unusually intelligent. But this is unlikely to happen if you focus on praising your child's effort, not his native ability. "Wow, you're smart!" is simply a comment about genetics. "Wow, you're really working hard at that!" puts success in a child's grasp.

Quality Time

My five-year-old's love language is quality time. Nothing makes her happier than a tea party or a round of board games or a game of hopscotch with mom. In fact, if at bedtime she realizes that we didn't find time in the day for at least two games, she reminds me that we'll need to play catch-up the next day.

Sometimes families think of movie time as quality time. That can be a fun thing to do together, but the problem with TV time is that it doesn't allow conversation and interaction. It should not compose the majority of your together time. Quality time is more than mere proximity.

Conversation time is essential for a good relationship. My oldest daughter is away at college, and we have a lot of conversation via e-mail. I've found that a great way to spark an interesting e-mail is to ask her about her "bests" and "worsts" for the day. This works for younger children too and is an excellent conversation generator at the dinner table.

Whether it's sitting on the couch for a cuddle and a chat or shooting hoops in the driveway, quality time is a love language that is shared by many. I have noticed a strong tendency for children to want time to talk with mom at bedtime. At the end of a long day, sometimes I just want to kiss the kids and go out to the living room for some quiet time with my husband. But slowing down to spend even three minutes talking with each child shows them I am committed to them and ends the day on a good note.

Receiving Gifts

All kids love to get gifts, but children with this love language really treasure the gifts that they receive. They see gifts as visible symbols of love. These kids probably also enjoy shopping and giving gifts, and are likely to come up with just the right gift for any occasion. One of my girls unfailingly gives the most beautifully decorated packages around. Every detail is perfect and carefully chosen.

Since this is not my love language, I have to remind myself of the importance of gifts to others. Luckily, this love language is one of the easiest to learn. Keep in mind, too, that gifts don't necessarily have to be expensive to be pleasing to the child whose love language is gifts. A small thing given thoughtfully and with love can be just as precious as something expensive.

A good example of this is a note from mom or dad. Mention specific things you enjoy about that child. I know that my own father loved me like crazy, but I don't have such a letter from him, and I wish I did. A thoughtfully written letter is a priceless gift.

Acts of Service

I never feel more loved than when someone offers to give me a hand with something on my to-do list. Even a simple thing like straightening a cupboard or scrubbing a sink can make me smile. If your child has this love language, he or she will probably be pleased if you pitch in and offer to work by his side or if you do something small that makes his life easier.

Try to notice what is most important to your child. Different people will want help with different things. If your teenager is feeling overwhelmed by school projects, ask him what he needs most. Would he rather you grab him a snack, proofread his essay, or buy him a new printer cartridge the next time you're at the store? Listening to your child's needs can really pay off in relationship building.

Physical Touch

Everyone needs touch, but if this is your child's primary love language, in times of stress, he will be comforted by touch more than anything else. Several of my boys respond to physical affection better than any other type of affection. Boys especially sometimes resist the "gooey" kind of cuddles, but their smiles light up the room at the suggestion of an arm wrestle or a tickling match.

Rocking in a rocking chair or on a lawn swing together is another great way to get in some touch and movement, even when you're not in the mood for rowdy play. In fact, there are some children who very much enjoy cuddles but steer far from rowdy play. Observe your child to learn what he or she enjoys most. Little acts such as a touch on the cheek or a quick hug as your child is running by are easy ways to work affection into the day, and tell your child how much he or she is loved by you.

After reading this section, you may be wondering if it is even possible to parent so intentionally all the time. No way. Just figuring out your child's love language will take awhile. But once you have a guess at what makes each of your children tick, set yourself a small goal. Aim for just one interaction per day per child, where you show him love in his own love language. Your child's reaction will tell you whether or not you've guessed his language. The positive feedback you get once you've got him pegged will likely encourage you to work in more interactions each day in his language.

What about Gender Differences?

People are so bent on being politically correct that they hesitate to even admit that there may be differences between the sexes. But any mother who has more than a kid or two knows that boys and girls are different.

Over the years, my older daughters and I have enjoyed passing a journal back and forth between us, writing notes about what has been going on in our lives. If I asked one of my boys to share a journal with me, they'd think I was trying to torture them. On the other hand, when I playfully slug one of my boys in the shoulder, his eyes light up: playtime! If I tried that move with one of my girls, they'd be full of righteous indignation. Sure, there are exceptions to the rule—people vary widely in their preferences, and, again, you need to be aware of what works for your particular child. But, in general, girls enjoy a different style of interaction than do boys.

One really effective method of encouraging boys towards good behavior is through the use of power words. Boys, big or small, admire power. There's a reason Spiderman is so popular with guys. They are biologically made to be the problem-solvers, the warriors, the rescuers.

That doesn't mean women are weak or that they can't solve problems. But I believe boys are biologically programmed to admire strength and to want to be strong themselves. If we as moms can steer boys to the strength of character it takes to make positive choices, they will be more likely to gravitate towards those choices.

If I have a son who is being tempted towards lying, I'll talk with him about being strong enough to tell the truth—about being a warrior for what's true and right and about not being fearful. If he's having trouble resisting the crowd, we'll talk about the strength it takes to be a leader rather than a follower. We talk about how choosing right builds his decision-making muscles to be stronger in the future.

Of course, we also need to help our boys understand and express their own feelings—they need to know it's okay to cry. But sometimes we moms forget that in each of our little boys there lurks a warrior, waiting to come out. If we can guide that warrior towards good, we will help him grow up strong.

Finding Time for One on One

In a busy household, it can be hard to find time for a good conversation.

> Scrapbooking offers another opportunity to
> celebrate my children as individuals.

But time for individual conversation with each child is at the heart of showing them how precious they are to you. Some of my most treasured memories from growing up the oldest of eight involve going out on errands with my mom. Having mom to myself, even just at the grocery store, was heaven.

I do this with my children as well. When I go shopping, I will often take just one or two children with me. When my husband runs to the hardware store or even to the dump, he takes a child. Errands don't have to be glamorous to allow conversation time in the car.

We also like to plan activities with children that both parents and children enjoy. My husband coaxes the kids to wash a car with him. I pull out a deck of cards. For awhile, I was working out on my treadmill every day. I discovered that the book rack on my treadmill was just big enough for a game of Phase Ten with one of my children. A whole game of Phase Ten lasted long enough for me to get in a couple of miles on the treadmill and was a great distraction as well as being a great time for bonding.

Scrapbooking offers another opportunity to celebrate my children as individuals. I love taking pictures. Over the years, I've begun a scrapbook for each of my children. I've worked on them gradually, and it is a fun thing for each child to have his or her own book to look at now and then. When each child turns ten, I present them with a batch of scrapbooking supplies, and at that point they can work on their scrapbooks on their own. Often, when I sit down at the dining room table to do some scrapbooking, one of my older kids will pull out their scrapbooking supplies and join me to work on their own album.

You may also like to plan a big outing with a child or two at a time. I've been able to take several of my older children on international trips as I've traveled to adopt the younger children. My oldest daughter and I went to Korea. I took my second and third children to Ethiopia, and I hope to take several other children to Korea in 2009.

Birthday Time!

Birthdays are the perfect time to show kids how much they mean to us. With ten kids, we have birthdays in every month except August and October. Despite the frequency of birthdays around our place, birthdays are celebrated with great love and enthusiasm. We've done a Korean barbecue in our backyard. We've done cake and ice cream and soccer with friends at the park. We've hosted a tea party for a dozen little girls. Occasionally, we throw a really big shindig, like the sit-down dinner for thirty when our eldest daughter turned eighteen.

But the vast majority of the time we celebrate in our own home with a homemade cake and as much of our extended family as can come on that day. Kids are allowed to invite a friend or two. We decorate the living room with balloons that we blow up ourselves. We make a cake of the child's choosing and stir up a pitcher of lemonade. Usually, at least a dozen or so relatives show up, which, along with the home crowd, makes for a good-sized gathering. In warm weather we'll sometimes put up the pool and ask guests to bring swimsuits. Sometimes there will be a scavenger hunt or a piñata. There are always treat bags for young guests to take home.

For us, this moderate approach is perfect. The big crowd of well-wishers makes each child feel special, and yet it's not really any more trouble to plan a party for thirty than it is to invite just three or four friends. The homemade party fare is affordable, and the varying ages of the guests mean that everyone can find someone to chat with. It is also less overwhelming for the birthday child to have just one or two friends to focus on, along with family. Sometimes when you invite the whole class, it can be hard to make sure that the birthday child spends time with each young guest.

John and I also take each child out for dinner sometime during the birthday week. The child gets to pick the restaurant and has mom and dad to himself. With only one child, John and I almost feel like we're getting a date ourselves, and it is a great time to catch up and have a nice conversation with the child.

Shannon, a mother of four from Arkansas, does something similar with her children:

> I have a date tonight with a blond-haired, brown-eyed cutie with a great laugh and an obsession with Anakin Skywalker. It's my eight-(and-a-half!)-year-old son, Stephen. Inspired by a similar tradition in my family growing up, we do a little half-birthday celebration in the Dryer house. On each of the kids' half birthdays, they get to go on a real live "date" with the opposite gender parent. I take the boys, and my husband will take Corrie when she's a little older. In our noisy, busy family, it's so special to set aside an evening like this, where the half-birthday-boy (or girl!) gets to choose the restaurant/movie, etc., for an entire evening, with one-on-one time with a parent. So tonight, Stephen and I are eating at a local restaurant that throws (actually THROWS!) the dinner rolls at you. Thankfully, Stephen's a better catcher than I am. Afterwards, we'll be yo-ho-ho-ing with Captain Jack Sparrow at the new Pirates of the Caribbean flick.

Shannon's idea reminds me of another of our birthday traditions. On the morning of their birthdays, we serve each of our children breakfast in bed. Each child gets to choose what he or she wants for breakfast. We set up a breakfast tray with all the fixings: fruit, condiments, coffee,

On the morning of their birthdays, we serve
each of our children breakfast in bed.

even for the littlest ones. Whether they actually like coffee or not, they all think it is cool to be offered it on their birthdays.

Once the tray is set up, the whole family parades into the birthday child's room with the tray, singing "Happy Birthday." Once the child is comfortably ensconced with breakfast, he or she is handed a bell with which to call for assistance at any point during the meal.

There are lots of moments in parenthood where you just have to go by guesswork and hope you got it right. But when we all parade singing into a child's room with that special birthday-breakfast tray, I know there's a moment we're getting right. Moments like these will live in our children's hearts for the rest of their lives.

> *"If I had my child to raise all over again,*
> *I'd build self-esteem first, and the house later.*
> *I'd finger-paint more, and point the finger less.*
> *I would do less correcting and more connecting.*
> *I'd take my eyes off my watch, and watch with my eyes.*
> *I'd take more hikes and fly more kites.*
> *I'd stop playing serious, and seriously play.*
> *I would run through more fields and gaze at more stars.*
> *I'd do more hugging and less tugging."*
> —Diane Loomans, from "If I Had My Child To Raise All Over Again"

CONCLUSION

Never Alone

I was a kindergartener, excited over my school's end-of-year program. I remember waiting for my mother to arrive and being so proud when I caught sight of her. She had my three younger siblings in tow and was pregnant with another. Though my siblings doubtless took much of her attention during that performance, she was there to clap and cheer, and that was enough for me.

In a big family, you're never alone.

A decade later, I was on my way to the mall with my family to buy my dad new shoes. There were eight kids by then. As we trundled across the parking lot, my folks, as always, were stopped by strangers wondering if all these children could possibly be theirs. "They're so well behaved!" exclaimed the woman. My parents glowed and I glowered, excruciatingly embarrassed. I thought longingly of my best friend's "perfect" family of two children and swore that I would never have more than four children.

In a big family, you're never alone.

Four years later, two months after my nineteenth birthday, I walked down the aisle in my mother's wedding dress behind five bridesmaids, two of whom were my sisters, as another sister played the cello in the choir loft above. The church was packed. My mother is one of six siblings, and our wedding was the first of this next generation on both sides of the family. We were the center of a mob of well-wishers.

In a big family, you're never alone.

A year and a half later came the birth of our first daughter, with more rejoicing and a playpen full of baby gifts for this young couple trying to get through college. I was three months from getting my nursing degree. I took twelve days off after my daughter's birth and went back to class. That first morning, trying to get the baby fed and changed and fed and changed, and myself dressed, and both of us out the door on time, it all seemed too hard. I burst into tears and called my mother. She was there in ten minutes. Three months later, thanks in part to grandma-provided child care, I graduated, just in time to put my husband through school.

In a big family, you're never alone.

When my oldest daughter was six months old, I got the terrible call from my sister. "Daddy was working on the car, and it fell on him, and he died." In a throat-clutching barefoot fog, I put my baby in her car seat and drove to be with my mother. On the way there, I was stunned that the world still hummed heartlessly along. I was barely twenty-one. My youngest sister was six. There were six children between us. We sat, stunned, in my mother's house as the doorbell rang over and over, and trays of food filled our kitchen, and wads of Kleenex clumped in our damp fists. That night, several of us slept in our mother's bed with her, and the rest filled beds in the house and overflowed to a tent in the yard. People wondered aloud how my mother would get along, with all my siblings to care for. She said through tears, chin stubbornly up, "I couldn't do it without them."

In a big family, you're never alone.

A decade later, heart changed by motherhood, I set aside my teenaged "no more than four kids" decree and flew with my husband to Korea to "birth" our fifth child, a four-month-old baby boy. Jubilation trumped exhaustion as we walked off that airplane, finally home after five days in a foreign country, to a raucously excited three dozen or so of our nearest and dearest.

In a big family, you're never alone.

Last summer, the airport scene was repeated for the fifth time. John and I stumbled bleary-eyed off the airplane, bringing home our ninth and tenth children. Balloons and banners and delighted relatives greeted these children just as joyfully as they had our first.

In a big family, you're never alone.

Two springs ago, we watched my grandfather begin to slip from this earth. Difficult decisions about his care were made in sotto voce group discussions, with the burden borne equally among his six children. In his last drifting-away hours, generation after generation rotated quietly through his room, singing "Jesus Loves Me" and holding his hand and whispering their love in his ear. Just after sunrise, he went home to heaven, trailed at the funeral by balloons released from the hands of his many great-grandchildren into the clear blue sky.

In a big family, you're never alone.

This spring, my second daughter graduated from high school, cheered on by a boisterous group of friends, parents, grandparents, siblings, aunts, uncles, and cousins.

In a big family, you're never alone.